START-TO-FINISH
JOB SEARCH
GUIDE

COLLEGE STUDENT EDITION

by
Richard Blazevich

This book is protected under the copyright laws of the United States of America. Any reproductions or other unauthorized use of the material herein is prohibited without the express written permission of the author.

Copyright © 2018 by Richard Blazevich
All rights reserved.

Amazing Job Skills Publishing Company
Dallas, Texas
www.AmazingJobSkills.com

Contents

1. Your Interview Group 5
2. Your Job Hunting Strategy 19
3. Your Resume 35
4. Your List of Interview Questions 51
5. Opening Questions 61
6. Fit Questions 81
7. Case Questions 105
8. Nail the Interviews 123

Conclusion 135
Reference Materials 143
Acknowledgements 201
About the Author 203

Introduction

Over the past twenty years, I've interviewed hundreds of college students. Most of them were bright and highly motivated. Very few of them had the interview skills needed to get the jobs they wanted.

In rare instances, I've interviewed students who were amazing. They gave compelling answers to all the questions they were asked, and they received offers from nearly every recruiter who interviewed them.

If you want to become one of those superstar job candidates, this book is for you. You'll find a game plan for dazzling recruiters with incredible answers to the toughest interview questions. You'll find tips for researching companies and figuring out exactly what their recruiters are looking for. And you'll find advice for refining your skills and using tools that are available to you on your college campus.

I used many of the techniques in this book when I was a student. When I first entered business school, my fellow students might have elected me "Least Likely to Succeed" if my school had such an award. I was awkward, and I had no experience in my chosen career field. By the time I finished my two-year program, I had gotten an

INTRODUCTION

internship at one of the best marketing companies in the world, and I received job offers from powerhouse companies, including Frito-Lay, General Mills, Kraft, SC Johnson, and Quaker.

Those impressive results didn't happen because I was talented. My natural ability paled in comparison to that of my fellow classmates. Those results happened because I learned the secrets to interviewing. This book will reveal those secrets to you.

As a college student, you'll spend years getting educated in your chosen subject matter. However, if you're like most students, you'll receive very little help to get the jobs you want.

When I was in college, I was lucky enough to get life-changing advice from my school's career counselors. Their coaching set me up for years of success in my career. Most students aren't so fortunate. They won't receive the guidance they need to get the jobs they want.

After graduation, I started recruiting students for my company's marketing department. I noticed that many of the most accomplished students didn't know how to answer interview questions. Their responses were often vague and didn't communicate their true potential. I knew that without strong interview skills, they would never make it through our rigorous selection process.

When I found particularly talented students who performed poorly during interviews, I offered them suggestions to improve their skills. That led to me organizing interview workshops for student organizations and career development offices at colleges where my company recruited.

In this book, I'll share the playbook I developed for those workshops. I'll also give you tips based on my years of experience recruiting students from some of the top universities in the world. My hope is that you'll learn from this advice so you'll get the interviews you want. Then, you'll nail those interviews using the skills you'll develop from the process described in this book.

To illustrate some of the concepts, I've included a story about four fictional college students who became successful at interviewing. While these specific students don't exist in the real world, they represent the combined experiences of many students who've gone through the job hunting process.

In each chapter, I'll summarize the key lessons from the story. I'll also provide tools and templates you can use

INTRODUCTION

to dramatically improve the skills you need to get job offers.

One more thing … if you've read my other book, *Amazing Interview Answers*, you'll notice that some of the content in this book is repeated from that one. Please forgive the duplication. You'll find that most of the content in this book will be new. The information that came from my other book helps me explain the game plan I recommend for interview preparation. I suggest you read this book first to build your strategy. Then, as you practice your answers to interview questions, use the *Amazing Interview Answers* book to help you refine your own amazing answers for the most commonly asked interview questions.

Now, let's get started.

1. Your Interview Group

When I was in school, I received the best career advice of my life. It happened when I asked a career counselor to tell me the most important thing I could do to get job offers. Without hesitation, she said four words that changed my life. I guarantee that if you follow those four words of advice, it will significantly increase your odds of getting job offers.

In the story you're about to read, I'll reveal the advice that became instrumental in my success.

As you read the story, keep in mind that your peers will be your best resource throughout your career. They're highly motivated to help you because you're going to help them. You'll find other resources, including career counselors, professors, and mentors, but your peers will have the most to offer you.

Let's see how the characters in our story approach their job hunting journey.

***

After his summer break, Jim Harrison arrived at Southern State University and started to panic. He seemed

1. YOUR INTERVIEW GROUP

behind all of his classmates. They were coming back from impressive summer jobs that gave them valuable experiences in their desired career fields. He was coming back from a summer job as a camp counselor, which paled in comparison to the summer jobs that his fellow students had.

Jim wanted to be a high-powered marketer someday. Since his first business class in high school, he knew marketing was the path for him. It just seemed impossible to get a good summer job at a reputable company.

The previous year, Jim always felt like he was behind. He didn't hear about most jobs until after the companies had finished their interviews. For the jobs he did hear about, he interviewed, but he wasn't given any offers.

As he walked into the student lounge, Jim saw Don from his track team. He went up to Don and shook his hand. "Hey, Don. How was your summer?"

"Hey, Jim. It was awesome. I got an internship at Titan Supercenters in their sales department. At the end of the summer, they gave me an offer to work there again next summer. They said that if everything goes well, they'll give me a full-time job when I graduate."

"That's great. It sounds like you're all set."

"Yeah, I really loved working there. And it'll make things so much easier if I don't have to worry about finding a job. How was your summer?"

Jim cringed. "It was OK."

Don looked sympathetic. "Where'd you work?"

"Actually, I was a camp counselor."

"What? I thought you wanted to be in marketing. Being a campy isn't gonna get you squat."

"Thanks for the encouragement, pal. Seriously, I don't know what I'm doing wrong. I tried to get a good summer job, but it didn't work out. What should I be doing differently?"

"Look, buddy, I'm gonna give you the best career advice you'll ever get. Are you ready?"

"Yep, lay it on me."

"Here it is. **Form an interview group**. That's what I did, and it was the best decision I've ever made. Well, gotta go. See you in the weight room tomorrow."

As Don turned and walked away, Jim called out, "Wait! What's an interview group?" Don must not have heard him as he rushed out of the student lounge.

Jim was left standing alone, wondering what "form an interview group" meant.

1. YOUR INTERVIEW GROUP

The next day, Jim ran into Emily from his debate club. She gave him a friendly hug and said, "Hey Jim, how've you been?"

"Great. I just got settled into my new apartment. How about you?"

She grinned. "I'm doing well. My summer was absolutely amazing! I interned at Hydropolypharm doing marketing projects for their new blood pressure medicine. My boss actually tried to get me to start working there full-time. She said I could be a marketing assistant while I finished my degree at night school. I told her I had to come back here full time to teach you how to be a better debater." Emily gave Jim a grin. "What did you do for the summer?"

"Actually, I was a camp counselor."

"What? I thought you were interested in marketing. Why didn't you get a marketing job?"

"I tried, but I couldn't find one."

"Jim, you're one of the smartest guys I know. Are you telling me that you couldn't find a single marketing job for the summer?"

"I appreciate the compliment ... I think. Things just didn't go my way. I always found out about jobs too late, or when I did get an interview, they'd give the job to someone else."

Emily gave Jim a sympathetic look. "That sucks. I hope you have better luck this year."

"Thanks. If you don't mind me asking, how'd you get your summer job?"

"It was easy. Someone from my interview group told me that Hydropolypharm was coming to campus to interview students, so I sent their recruiter my resume. They put me on their interview list, and, well, I nailed the interview."

"Someone from your interview group? What's an interview group?"

"Come on, Jim. You gotta be kidding. You're not in an interview group? No wonder you didn't get a good summer job. An interview group is the key to finding good jobs. It'll help you get your resume ready, help you research jobs, and most importantly, help you practice interviewing."

"How do I get into an interview group?"

"That's easy. Just form one yourself. Find a few people, and set up meetings with them. Come to think of it, I have a friend who's transferring here from Northern State University, and she's not in an interview group yet. Maybe she can join yours. Her name is Sarah. I'll text you

1. YOUR INTERVIEW GROUP

her phone number." Emily looked at her watch. "I'm late for class. Gotta go."

"Wait. I need you to tell me more about interview groups."

"No time. Just go to the career development office. They'll tell you everything you need to know." Emily hurried off to class.

Again, Jim was left standing alone wondering why everyone seemed to know about interview groups but him. He pulled up the campus directory on his phone and found the career development office.

Later that afternoon, Jim walked into their office and found the receptionist sitting at a desk near the front door. "Hi, I'm Jim Harrison. I'd like to talk with someone about forming an interview group."

"Great, one of our career counselors will be right with you."

Jim sat in the waiting room feeling hopeful. It seemed like the secrets of getting a good job were about to be revealed. Whatever an interview group was, it might be the key to his future success.

After waiting a few minutes, Jim heard someone call out, "Jim Harrison?" He looked up and saw Billy, one of the camp counselors who helped train him a few summers ago.

Jim stood up and shook Billy's hand. "Hey, Billy. What are you doing here?"

"I guess I'm your career counselor. They said you wanted to talk about interview groups."

"That's right. Honestly, I don't even know what an interview group is, but it seems to be something that can help me get a good job."

"Well, you've come to the right place. Interview groups are my specialty." Billy led Jim past the receptionist to a small cubicle.

As they sat down, Billy said, "Let me start by explaining what an interview group is. They typically have three to five people who meet several times a week, and their goal is to help their members build the skills needed to get the best jobs possible."

"Why are there only three to five members? That seems like a small group."

"It's so you can work around each other's schedules. If you get too many members, it's hard to find times when you all can meet."

"How do you find people to be in the group?"

1. YOUR INTERVIEW GROUP

"That's the easy part. Just pick some of your friends or classmates. Think of people you've worked with on group projects or in clubs. Tell them what you're doing, and see if they want to join you. If people join, but they don't show up, don't worry about it. As long as you consistently get two or three other people at your meetings, you'll be fine."

"Should everyone have the same major?"

"Well, that's up to you. Some people like to be in groups with others in the same career field so you can share information about potential employers. Other people prefer to be in groups with people who have different majors so they don't feel like they're competing with their group members for the same jobs. It's your call."

"So, what should we do in our meetings?"

"First, you'll need to build your strategy. That means figure out which companies you want to interview with, how to network with their recruiters, and how to get on their interview schedules.

"Next, exchange resumes and give each other advice for making them better. That should take about a week or two.

"Then get a list of interview questions. We have lists here at the career development office, and some of the student organizations have good lists, too.

"Finally, practice your interview answers, give each other feedback, and repeat. You'll want to spend weeks practicing your answers and giving each other tips for making each answer better."

Jim nodded. "How often should we meet?"

"I recommend two or three times a week. That'll be often enough to get some good practice in your meetings, and you'll have enough time between meetings to practice on your own. Each meeting should last at least an hour, but not more than two hours."

"That's a lot of time. I'm not sure I have that much time to spare."

Billy paused, then asked, "Why did you come to college?"

Jim looked confused. "Same reason as everyone else. I want to get a good job."

"How's that working for you?"

"Not very well."

"You run track, right? How much time do you spend on that?"

1. YOUR INTERVIEW GROUP

"During the season, I spend a couple of hours a day, five or six days a week. In the off-season, maybe half that. I'm guessing that's a few hundred hours a year."

"How many years have you been running track?"

"Since I was in eighth grade, so that's six or seven years."

"So, to be competitive at track, you've spent over a thousand hours practicing. How many hours have you spent practicing your job interview skills?"

"That's not a fair comparison. The competition in track is fierce, and coaches expect me to practice a lot."

"OK. You've practiced for track because of your coaches, but you haven't practiced your job skills because no one expects you to. Which is more important, doing well in track or getting a good job?"

"Getting a good job."

"So, why aren't you willing to spend a few hours a week building the skills you need to be competitive in the job market? Look, I came to college for the same reasons as you, to get an education, play sports, party, and find a good job. After getting here, I heard a great story that taught me how to prioritize those things.

"A CEO hires a consultant to help him figure out how to improve his business. The CEO meets with the consultant and starts talking about his priorities. He explains that he wants to generate a profit for his investors, he wants to set the business up for long term success, and he wants to create an environment where employees will want to work.

"The consultant politely nods while the CEO talks. When the CEO finishes, the consultant asks to see the CEO's day planner. The CEO hands over the planner, and the consultant spends a few minutes flipping through it. Then the consultant says, 'Now I'm going to tell you what your priorities really are. Your top priority is to socialize with other executives. Your second priority is to travel to interesting places. Your third priority is to spend time with the people who're planning your company's holiday party. You see, your priorities aren't what you say they are. Your priorities are what your calendar says they are.'

"The consultant was right. You said your top priority is to get a good job, but how much of your time do you spend on that? You need to put your money where your mouth is ... or rather, put your time where your priorities are. If your top priority is to get a good job, you should spend more time preparing for that. The best way to prepare is to form that interview group and use it to practice for your job skills."

Jim looked down. "I've never thought of it that way. It seems like I've been wasting my time on the wrong things."

Billy shrugged. "Probably. The good news is that you still have time left. The question is what'll you do with it."

Jim left the career development office committed to forming his interview group and getting started on his job hunting game plan. Over the next few days, he thought about who he'd like to get in his group. He wanted to find people who were motivated and people he enjoyed spending time with. He decided that he'd find people who were majoring in different subjects so he wouldn't feel like he was competing with them for the same jobs.

In the end, Jim invited Ethan, his best friend from high school, who was majoring in computer science. He also invited Abby, who he knew from the track team. She was majoring in engineering. Jim did contact Sarah, who was recommended to him by his debate team colleague Emily. Sarah was getting a dual degree in nursing and psychology.

When they compared class schedules, they found that everyone was available on Mondays, Wednesdays, and Fridays from 11:00 a.m. to noon, so they reserved those times for their meetings. They agreed to meet in a quiet corner of the student lounge.

***

It's rare that we spend much time doing things that we consider to be our top priorities. Most students spend the majority of their time in classes, socializing, and in extra-curricular clubs or sports. Very little time is spent on making ourselves marketable to future employers.

One issue is that we're not accountable to anyone for building our career skills. We feel more accountable to professors, friends, coaches, and team members so we spend our time on things they want us to do.

If your goal is to get a job in a competitive field, you should make yourself accountable for building the skills you'll need to get the job you want. An interview group is a perfect way to build that accountability. If you form an interview group and commit to meeting with your fellow group members who rely on you to build their skills, you'll stand a better chance of following through.

Interview groups shouldn't seem like an obligation. They should be fun. You should find people you enjoy spending time with and people who bring out the best in you. Look for people who are motivated so your time is productive, but also look for people you enjoy being with.

If you don't know where to find people for your interview group, you have several options. Student organizations are a great place to start. Even if they don't currently offer interview groups, you can encourage a student organization to add this service to their list of activities. Interview groups would be great offerings for academic organizations such as marketing clubs or math clubs. They would also be great for fraternities, sororities, and diversity clubs. You can also see if your career development office or a professor can help you get into an interview group.

Once you form your group, commit to specific days and times to meet each week. I recommend meeting three times a week for at least an hour per meeting. That'll give you enough time to practice without it being a burden.

You should also commit to a certain amount of time to practice by yourself between meetings. I recommend you schedule two to three hours a week to do that.

See page 145 for a template to help you plan your interview group.

2. Your Job Hunting Strategy

After you've formed your interview group, it'll be time to build your job hunting strategy. Like any strategy, this involves defining your goals, identifying your options, and picking the best option to get the results you want.

I recommend you start by spending some time looking over a variety of job descriptions just to make sure you understand the type of work you're getting into. Unfortunately, students typically aren't required to understand job duties before picking a major in college. Sometimes your courses will give you an idea of what's involved in your future career, but often they won't.

I started my career in accounting, which was absolutely the wrong choice for me. I picked it because I enjoyed business and I wanted job security. While accounting was a good fit for those two criteria, if I had read a job description for an accountant, I would have heard sirens go off in my head telling me to avoid that career.

A typical accounting job description includes words like organize, verify, and audit, which are all things I hate doing. If I had read through a few other job descriptions, I

2. YOUR JOB HUNTING STRATEGY

might have stumbled across my real calling, which is marketing. I might have found a job description with words like create, lead, and develop, which are things I love doing.

There's actually an outstanding government website with hundreds of useful job descriptions. Yes, you heard that right ... an outstanding government website. Who would have thought?

I recommend you spend a few minutes on the U.S. government's site for the Bureau of Labor Statistics. The website address is www.bls.gov/ooh. The "o.o.h." stands for Occupational Outlook Handbook. I know that sounds incredibly boring, and while it's not the most entertaining site in the world, the content is extremely helpful.

On that site, you can find mini job descriptions for hundreds of careers. If the duties for your chosen field get you excited, you're on the right path. If they make you cringe, start searching for other options. You might be in the right general area, like business was the right area for me, but you might be looking at the wrong specific job, like accounting was wrong for me.

If nothing in your chosen career field gets you excited, that's OK. You may be in the wrong field. It's better to figure that out now than to figure it out after you graduate and start working, like I did. Hopefully, once you've spent some time surfing around the Occupational Outlook Handbook, you'll find a job description that gets you excited, or at least puts a smile on your face. If not, go directly to your school's career development office. They have people who are trained to help you find your dream career. You've already paid their fees through your tuition, so you might as well use their services.

When you find the job that excites you, it'll be time to plan your strategy. The first step is setting your goal. That should be easy. Your goal could be to get a summer job with a great company in the line of work you want.

Next, you should define your options. That might take a little longer. It involves finding companies to target for your job hunting. College campuses are full of resources to help you do this. You can start with your career development office. The career counselors there should have lists of companies that recruit for each major offered by your college. They can also tell you which of those companies come to campus and when they conduct their interviews.

Most career development offices and alumni relations departments also keep track of where previous students are currently working. You can use that

2. YOUR JOB HUNTING STRATEGY

information to find companies that are likely to hire students from your college.

Professors are another great resource for job hunting. Many of them have relationships with companies that come to campus. As a recruiter, when I'm looking for top candidates, I often start by asking professors which students might be a good fit for my company. If you tell your professors what you're looking for, they can be your best advocates with potential employers.

Student organizations can also be invaluable. When I was looking for a marketing internship, my school's marketing club had already created a list of companies that recruited at our school. That list included names of the recruiters, dates for their campus visits, and how many summer interns they've hired in the past. It also included some fun facts about each company like which ones were process-oriented and which ones had a culture that was more entrepreneurial. This information was invaluable for me since I was rebelling against the process-oriented field of accounting.

Finally, don't forget to ask your friends, classmates, and interview group members. Some of them may know about great employers. When I was in business school, many of my hallway conversations were about companies that I'd like to work for and when those companies might be interviewing on campus.

Now it's time for you to start building your short list of potential employers. Look for companies that have a history of hiring summer interns from your school. As you build your list, take notes on key attributes for each company. Your notes should include the names of their recruiters, when they conduct their interviews, how many people they've hired in the past, what their company culture might be like ... things like that.

Next, you should prioritize those companies based on what's most important to you. Here are the criteria I used to prioritize my prospects:

- how well-respected the company is,
- how unstructured the company is, and
- if I think I'd be a good fit with the culture.

Your criteria might be different based on what's important to you. That's OK. You should rank potential employers based on your specific priorities.

When you have your list of prioritized companies, it'll be time for you to plan your interview schedule. You should have a calendar of dates showing when each company will be on campus and when you want to interview with them. If they conduct on-campus interviews, their campus-visit dates should be available through your career development office. If not, feel free to contact each company's recruiters directly. Recruiters enjoy receiving politely written emails asking for information. It can be as simple as introducing yourself, telling them that you're interested in their company, and asking them when their interviews will be.

That's all it takes to build a strategy. It may seem like a lot, but think of it as a game of hide-and-seek. All the information you need is hidden somewhere. Your job is to seek it out. Depending on how good your career development office, student organizations, and friends are at providing information, you might be able to build a good list of prospective employers in less than a week.

Let's see how the characters in our story approach this stage of the job hunting process.

* * *

Jim was feeling good about his newly formed interview group. All three of his fellow members seemed eager to dive into the challenge of finding amazing summer jobs. He tried to remember what Billy, his career counselor, said to do next. Was it something about building his job hunting strategy? If so, what did that mean? Jim decided to give Billy a visit.

Jim stopped at the career development office and scheduled an appointment with Billy later that day. When he came back a few hours later, Billy gave him a stern look. "You better be here to tell me that you've formed your interview group."

Jim grinned. "Not only did I form an interview group, but it's the best interview group on campus. We're all set and ready to go. I'm here to figure out what we do next."

"Great," Billy said. "This is my favorite part … well, my second favorite part. My favorite part is opening all the emails with the job offers. My second favorite part is building a job hunting strategy. Here's how it works. You're gonna create a list of companies that you might want to work for. I'll start you off with our list of companies that come to campus to hire marketers. Then, I want you to do some research on those companies as well as others you might find."

Billy pulled up a file on his laptop. "OK, here's our list of marketing companies." He showed Jim the screen. "We have ten companies on our list. It looks like we don't have much information about them. Record keeping is not our strong point. We lost part of our database last year, so we're just starting to rebuild our employer info. I'll email you this list, and you can add to it as you go."

"How do I find other companies?" Jim asked.

"You're in luck. There's a great marketing club at your business school. They're one of the best student clubs at collecting information about employers. Get their list of companies and bring it back to me. We can go through it together."

"Great. Is there anything else I should do before our next meeting?"

"Yeah, I want you to ask your professors and classmates about companies that might be good job prospects. Plus, you might want to stop by the alumni office to see if they'll give you a list of people who graduated from here and are working in marketing jobs. On that list, they should include the names of companies where those people work."

Jim was starting to feel overwhelmed. "That's a lot of work."

"Yep. This is the part of the process that takes the most research. You'll be surprised how easy it is once you get started, especially if your marketing club has already done the work for you or if you find a helpful professor who's good at networking with recruiters."

Before they ended their meeting, Billy and Jim scheduled weekly meetings to review Jim's progress and discuss next steps. Billy concluded by saying, "Now, go get me a list of companies."

Jim met with his interview group the next morning and told them what he had learned from Billy.

Sarah was the first to respond. "That makes sense. My biggest problem has been that I didn't know where to start. I like the idea of having a list of companies to work from."

Ethan was next. "I don't know. So I have to go to the career development office, the alumni association, my computer science club, my professors, and my classmates. I really don't want a full-time job looking for a full-time job."

Abby looked to Ethan. "I don't think you have to go to all those places. I'm gonna start with my engineering club. Engineering students are ridiculously organized, so it wouldn't surprise me if our club has a good list of employers. You might want to start with the computer science club and see what they have."

2. YOUR JOB HUNTING STRATEGY

They all agreed to see what lists of companies they could find and report back at their next meeting.

Jim looked up the marketing club in his student directory and found out that Emily, his friend from the debate team, was one of the officers. He called Emily.

"Hey Em, this is Jim. You've been holding out on me."

"What do you mean?" Emily asked in a confused voice.

"I told you that I needed help finding a good marketing job, and you're in the marketing club. Doesn't the club have a list of companies that hire students from here?"

"Oops, I completely forgot about that," Emily admitted. "I suppose you'd like a copy of that list."

"I suppose I would. Do you know how I can get it?"

"Actually, yes. It's on our club's website. Let me pop on there, download a copy, and email it to you."

"Great. Any idea when you can do that?"

"I'm doing it as we speak. It should be in your inbox in three ... two ... one."

Jim opened his laptop and checked his email. He saw the subject line "Marketing Recruiters" at the top of his inbox. He opened the attachment and scanned the list. It included dozens of companies, along with the names of recruiters and interview dates for each company.

"Emily!" he shouted into the phone. "This is awesome! Why didn't you give me this list last year?"

"I didn't know it existed. I just found out about it during our club meeting last week. Honestly, I haven't even looked at it yet. Is it really that good?"

"It's beyond good. It's like getting a map to a buried treasure. You're the best! I owe you big for this."

"In that case, I need to think of a way you can repay me."

"You name it. Whatever you want."

"I do have one favor to ask. Can you be extra nice to my friend Sarah? She doesn't know many people since she's new here. Maybe you can spend some time with her to make her feel welcome."

"You got it. I'll see her at our next interview group meeting. Maybe I can show her around campus."

"Sounds great. That's all the payment I need," Emily said as she hung up the phone.

At their next interview group meeting, Jim shared his list of companies that hired marketers from their school. Each group member also shared their lists ... except Ethan.

Jim looked surprised. "Ethan, where's your list?"

"I didn't get around to it. I heard that software companies don't have their interviews until next semester, so I have plenty of time."

Jim shrugged. "If that's how you want to do things, that's your choice. The rest of us are gonna keep going since our interviews start earlier."

Sarah broke in. "Jim, let's go through your list and see what's on it."

They looked a Jim's list together, and he explained what he knew about each company. He also described the criteria he would to use to prioritize the companies. "I want a company that has a reputation for great marketing. It should also have a collaborative culture since I like working in groups."

Abby chimed in. "Maybe we should create a top tier and a bottom tier for your companies. The top tier will be ones that are the best fit for you. The bottom tier might be unknown companies or the companies that don't do marketing as well."

Jim smiled. "Love it. I'll do some research and come to our next meeting with my company list sorted into tiers."

Abby and Sarah agreed to do the same. Ethan said he might work on it, but he had a lot of other things to do that week.

After the meeting ended and Ethan left, Abby turned to Jim. "Doesn't it bother you that Ethan isn't taking this seriously?"

"Not really," Jim responded. "My dad used to have a saying: 'Run with the runners, and walk with the walkers.' Sometimes Ethan's a walker. He might not want to run as fast as we do, but he's a good guy. When he wants to engage, we'll be there for him. In the meantime, I'd like to keep running. Are you with me?"

"Absolutely. I'm worried about not having any good job prospects when I graduate. This interview group is the best thing I've got going. You, Sarah, and I can be runners. I guess I'm OK if Ethan decides to walk."

Jim thought to himself, "I just hope he doesn't stand on the sidelines until it's too late."

By the end of the week, Jim, Sarah, and Abby each had a list of their priority companies. Their lists included the contact information for each company's recruiters as well as dates when they'd be conducting interviews.

* * *

2. YOUR JOB HUNTING STRATEGY

As you see from our fictional story, building a job hunting strategy may seem intimidating at first. However, there are plenty of shortcuts. College campuses are full of information about employers, and you can fast-track your strategy by finding that information.

My favorite places to look are career development offices. The quality of information in these offices varies widely by college. Some have amazing lists of employers, complete with detailed information about recruiters, interview dates, job descriptions, and more. Others have very little information.

If your college's career development office doesn't have the information you need, try the other options that Billy recommended. See if your school's alumni office, student organizations, or professors have lists of potential employers. You may even find good lists that are maintained by upperclassmen, fraternities, or sororities. Don't be ashamed to ask around for this information. Most people who have found information about employers love to share it.

The internet is also full of information about potential employers. A simple online search may reveal hundreds of sites with details about companies that are hiring in your desired career field.

Now, start building your list of potential employers and prioritize them based on the criteria that are important to you.

See the Reference Materials section in the back of this book for a template to help you build your job hunting strategy.

2. YOUR JOB HUNTING STRATEGY

3. Your Resume

Once you have your list of prioritized companies, it's time to update your resume. There's a secret to doing this. Most employers have job descriptions for positions they're trying to fill. Get a few of those job descriptions from your top tier companies. That'll give you a great starting point to build your powerhouse resume. Those job descriptions are also the key to building your interview answers, but we'll get to that later.

Getting job descriptions is like getting answers to tests before you have to take the tests. In job descriptions, employers tell you exactly what they want to see on your resume and what they want to hear during interviews.

Finding job descriptions should be easy. Start by going to the best place for every step in your job hunting process. That's right, your career development office. They should have job descriptions from companies that recruit on your campus. If not, check online. Most big companies post job descriptions in the careers sections of their websites. If you can't find them there, try contacting the recruiters or human resources departments at those companies. Typically, they're willing to send job descriptions to interested candidates.

Once you have a few job descriptions, start circling the key action words on them like "design, create, analyze, and write." Employers love seeing words from their job descriptions repeated back to them on resumes. It shows that you understand the type of work to be done and you have experience doing it.

If you already have a draft of your resume, put it next to one of your targeted job descriptions. Check to see how well your bullet points match the duties on the job description. If the job description says that you'll be leading cross-functional teams, your resume should list any experience you have leading cross-functional teams. If the job description says that the company wants someone to design engineering specifications, your resume should include any experience you have designing engineering specifications.

Typically, people write their resumes based on the amount of time they spent on the tasks in their previous jobs. I once had a candidate who was looking for a job doing consumer research. On his resume, he included that he worked at the Salvation Army. He listed his experiences as folding clothes and cleaning the store. While he worked there, he also interviewed clients to see what types of services they might need. When I asked him why he didn't include that experience on his resume, he said that he spent most of his time folding clothes, not interviewing clients. We re-wrote his resume to feature his experience interviewing clients and assessing their needs since that was much more relevant for the consumer research job he wanted.

Employers don't care about your time allocation on previous jobs. They care about the relevant experience you gained and the results you delivered. Interviewing clients is extremely relevant for a consumer research role. Folding clothes is not. As a marketing recruiter, I didn't want a candidate who knew how to fold clothes. I wanted a candidate who could "conduct consumer research to assess the needs of potential customers," which is exactly what I had listed on the job description. I told that candidate to re-write his resume and include that relevant experience. I understood that it might not have been his primary duty, but it was the most relevant experience he had from that job.

You should go through your work history and think about experiences you've had that are most relevant for the job you want. Write those experiences in brief phrases that match the job description language as closely as possible. That's what employers want to see. Again, we don't care how much time you spent on each task. We care about the relevant experience you gained and the results you got.

Recruiters love to see numbers on resumes, so make sure you include as many measurable results as possible. If your actions resulted in a $50,000 increase in sales, include that on your resume. If you did something that saved your organization $5,000, include that. If you created a process that reduced the time to complete tasks by 20%, put that on your resume.

We also love to see awards, promotions, and leadership positions. You should include any relevant awards and contests you've won. For example, if you're going into engineering and you've won first place in a science fair, include that. If you were selected as employee of the month, include that. If you were elected to be your class treasurer, that's perfect, especially if you're applying for an accounting job.

Finally, I love to see some unusual things listed in the Additional Information section of a resume. If you have an unusual hobby, include it. That will let the recruiter know you might be more interesting than other candidates. I have to admit, I once agreed to interview someone just because they listed storm-chasing as one of their interests.

The rest of his resume wasn't impressive, but I really wanted to ask him about storm chasing.

I also love to see interests that show dedication. Examples include running marathons, completing Eagle Scout certification, and climbing mountains. If someone can complete those challenges, I feel like they'll be more likely to complete challenging work assignments.

I recommend you keep your resume to one page. Resumes that are several pages typically include too much unrelated content or are too repetitive.

The best resumes I've seen have four sections on a single page:

- **Contact Information**: Here, you should put your name, mailing address, email address, and phone number.
- **Education**: This will include your university, your degree, your graduation date, and key activities like student organizations and sports.
- **Experience**: Here, you should list the two or three most relevant jobs for the career you want. Include a few short bullet points for each job.
- **Additional Information**: This is where you should list any major awards, volunteer

positions, hobbies, certifications, and key accomplishments outside of work.

Remember, don't get too wordy and don't include things that are unrelated to the job that you want … other than a few eye-catching interests. If I'm looking through dozens of resumes, I'll choose the ones that are short and to the point.

Let's see what the characters in our story do to polish their resumes.

**

Jim went back to the career development office for his weekly meeting with Billy. Jim handed Billy a piece of paper and said, "Hey, Billy, here's my list of targeted companies."

Billy reviewed the list, asked a few questions, and gave his approval. "Let's move to the next step: polishing your resume. Let me see what your resume looks like."

Jim handed over a three-page list of jobs, skills, and interests. Billy grimaced. "This is a mess."

Jim frowned. "Don't sugar coat things. Tell me how you really feel."

"Sorry. I'm sure there's some good information here somewhere, but there's also a lot of junk. We're gonna get this down to one page with only the information that recruiters will care about. Let me show you an example."

Billy printed two pages and handed them to Jim. "The first page is the job description for the internship I had last summer. The second page is the resume I used to get that job."

Written on the first page was the job title "Summer School Teaching Assistant" along with job duties that included tutoring students and assisting teachers with lesson planning.

The second page was a copy of Billy's resume. It was well-organized and easy to read. *To see a copy of Billy's resume, go to the "Reference Materials" section in the back of this book.*

Jim looked over Billy's resume. "Wow. That's the shortest resume I've ever seen. Doesn't it make it seem like you have very little experience?"

"Actually, no. Recruiters don't care as much about the quantity of experience you have; they care about the quality. You'll notice that all my bullet points match up with the duties on the job description. The job duties include tutoring students, so on my resume, I list the experience I have tutoring students. It also lists helping with lesson planning, so my resume says … you guessed it … helping with lesson planning. That's a trick I use. I look at the job description, and I list all the experiences I have that relate to the duties on that job description.

"In the job descriptions, recruiters tell you exactly which skills they're looking for. You just have to repeat those skills back to them on your resume."

Jim nodded. "I think I get what you're saying."

"Good. Now do you have a job description for any of your targeted companies?"

Jim handed over a job description for his top priority company, Smitty's Automotive Brands, which was the largest retailer of car parts in the country. Billy scanned the page. "Good. This job description is very clear. I want you to take it and write your resume to include only your experiences that relate to the duties on it." Billy gave Jim a few more tips and sent him on his way.

At the next interview group meeting, Jim shared the information he had received from Billy. "Billy's recommendation is that we spend this week helping each other polish our resumes. Is everyone OK with that?" Everyone agreed.

When they exchanged resumes, they noticed that they each used different formats. Abby's resume was four pages, and it was written in paragraphs. Jim's was three pages with a lot of details about each job. Ethan didn't have a resume since he spent summers working at his family's store. Sarah had the shortest resume, which was only one page. It was clear, organized, and full of well-written bullet points.

"Wow," Abby said to Sarah. "I really like your resume. How did you write it?"

Sarah smiled. "Thanks. I found a great book with tips for writing resumes. I'll bring it to our next meeting."

Sarah explained the principles she used from that book. She organized her resume into sections called Education, Experience, and Additional Information. In the Education section, she listed the dual-degree she was working on, along with her anticipated graduation date. She also included her position as vice president of the university's healthcare club.

Under Experience, she listed two jobs in order from most recent to least recent. "My most recent job was this summer when I volunteered as a nursing assistant at a psychiatric hospital. I used action words to describe that experience, and I tried to quantify my results as much as possible."

Under the job title Summer Nursing Assistant, Sarah had written "Measured vital signs and medical histories for over 200 patients" and "Designed and implemented new check-in process that reduced patient waiting times by 30%".

For her other job, Sarah listed her experiences in similar fashion.

"The resume book said that recruiters love to see leadership positions on resumes, so if you've been an officer in a club or captain of a sports team, you should include that."

Ethan asked, "Why did you include things in the Additional Information section that have nothing to do with nursing?"

Sarah smiled. "Those are ice-breakers. I included them because I'm hoping recruiters will see something we have in common."

"Really?" Abby asked. "Do you think your interests in cooking and tennis have anything to do with getting a nursing job?"

"No, but the person who interviewed me for my last job also played tennis," Sarah said. "It gave us a common interest to talk about, which made the interview go more smoothly."

Next, the group reviewed Abby's resume. Sarah asked, "Is there a reason you wrote everything in paragraph format?"

Abby looked nervous. "Not really. I'm on the school newspaper staff, so I'm used to writing in paragraphs."

Sarah looked surprised. "You're on the newspaper staff? Why didn't you put that on your resume?"

"It doesn't have anything to do with engineering."

"I think it might. Don't engineers write reports and prepare presentations?"

"I don't know. To be honest, I'm not really sure what engineers do. I went into engineering because I'm good at math and I like designing things."

Jim said, "Billy told me the best way to write a resume is to get job descriptions for the jobs we want. Then, we should highlight our experiences that are most relevant based on those job descriptions."

Ethan started typing on his laptop. "Here's a job description for an engineer. It says that some of the responsibilities include writing bid proposals, environmental impact studies, and property descriptions."

Abby moved to Ethan's side and looked at his computer screen. "Let me see that. Hmm. It also says that engineers design project budgets. I'm the treasurer for my physics club. Maybe I should include that on my resume."

The group spent the next few days reviewing job descriptions and re-writing their resumes. When they finished, they all had well-organized, one-page resumes that highlighted their most relevant experiences for the jobs they wanted. They put their targeted job descriptions next to their resumes to ensure each resume delivered on the key job responsibilities.

On Jim's updated resume, he included bullet points with key words from the Smitty's Auto Brands job description including analyzed data, led cross-functional teams, and conducted research.

Sarah looked at Jim's resume. "This looks so much better. Since your experiences line up with the duties on the job description, their recruiters can see that you've done the type of work they're hiring for."

Jim looked over Abby's resume and said, "Now it's much easier to see what you've done. With your last resume, I felt like I was reading a book. With this version, I can glance at it and quickly see highlights of what you've done."

Since Ethan didn't have a resume to start with, the group spent extra time helping him. They asked him questions about his experiences, and they took notes on his responses. While he originally seemed disinterested in building his job hunting strategy, Ethan really enjoyed writing his resume.

At their next meeting, Ethan said, "Sorry I came unprepared last week. I didn't know where to start, so I kept putting things off. Now that I've found some good job descriptions, I feel like I'm getting the hang of this."

Abby gave Ethan a playful shove. "That's alright. Jim thought you might not come through, but I knew you had it in you."

The group members took one last look at each other's resumes, made a few final revisions, and agreed that the resumes were ready for prospective employers.

To see the resumes for the characters in this story, go to the "Reference Materials" section in the back of this book. You can also find a resume template on my website. Just go to www.AmazingJobSkills.com and click on the "Templates" link on the menu at the top of the home page.

* * *

3. YOUR RESUME

Now that the characters in our story have polished their resumes, let's review why a good resume is so important.

Resumes are typically the first impression recruiters will have of you. You want to present yourself as a compelling and relevant choice for the job they're trying to fill.

I've seen thousands of resumes over the years, and many of them were far too long. Often, job candidates included details about every job they've ever had. That's completely unnecessary. Recruiters don't want to see your life history. They just want to see what you've done that's related to the role they're trying to fill.

Another major issue with resumes is a lack of relevant information. I love to see resumes that make it clear the candidates understand the position they're applying for. Resumes do this when they list experiences relevant to the specific role without including unrelated information.

The secret to a great resume can be found in a job description. In the job description, employers are telling you exactly what they're looking for. They want to interview candidates who have experience related to the job duties for their open roles. You just need to write your resume to include those relevant experiences.

Obviously, you should never fabricate experiences that you don't have. You should always be truthful with everything you put on your resume. I've seen candidates put inaccurate or exaggerated information on their resumes. When I've asked them detailed questions about their experiences during interviews or when I've done fact-checking with their previous employers, the truth comes out. When it does, I immediately remove those candidates from consideration.

If a recruiter suspects that you've been untruthful on your resume or during an interview, the consequences could be severe. They could report you to your school for disciplinary action, or they could immediately remove you from consideration for their job. If, after they hire you, they find out you had inaccurate information on your resume, they will have grounds to fire you immediately.

If you feel like you have no relevant experiences for the job you want, that's OK. Now is the time to get those experiences. You can find a part-time job while you're in school to build your credentials. Again, start with the job description for your top priority position, then look for jobs that will give you experiences like those on that job description.

If you can't find a paying job that gives you relevant experience, try a volunteer position. There are thousands of organizations that need volunteers. You can contact them, tell them the type of experience you need, and ask them if they can use help in that area.

One of the best things you can do for your career is to study job descriptions for the type of career you want. Then, find jobs or projects that give you experiences related to those job descriptions. Those experiences can be in paying jobs, in volunteer positions, or in student organizations.

If you need ideas for finding relevant experiences, talk to your friends, family members, interview group counterparts, professors, or career counselors. Then, go get that experience and put it on your resume.

See page 149 for templates and examples to help you build your winning resume.

4. Your List of Interview Questions

Next is the easiest step in the job hunting process: getting a list of interview questions.

If getting a job description is like getting the answers to a test ahead of time, getting a good list of interview questions is like getting the questions to the test. It may seem like having a list of interview questions will give you an unfair advantage over other candidates, but as a recruiter, I don't mind when candidates prepared for my questions ahead of time. In fact, it shows that the candidate has a sincere interest in my company and they're willing to do their homework before an interview. Most recruiters appreciate that level of commitment.

To get a list of interview questions, go to my website, AmazingJobSkills.com, and click on the "Templates" link that's in the menu at the top of the page. The list on that site includes general questions that are commonly asked in interviews for a wide variety of career fields. If you're in a highly competitive, specialized field like medicine, consulting, or engineering, I encourage you to find a list of questions that are specific to your field. You can still use the questions on my website to practice your basic skills, but you may also want to practice using additional industry-specific questions that you find yourself.

For those questions, I recommend you start where you should start for most of your job hunting needs. That's right, your school's career development office. They should have a list of questions commonly asked in your career field. If not, many student organizations give lists of interview questions to their members. When I was in business school, our marketing club had a list of the fifty most commonly asked questions in marketing interviews. We even updated that list annually based on the questions we heard from recruiters each year.

Most interviews will include three types of questions: opening questions, fit questions, and case questions.

Opening Questions: The most common question in an interview is "tell me about yourself." This is the recruiter's way of seeing if you can communicate relevant information about yourself. Your response to this question will set the tone for the rest of the interview. If you nail it, you'll start with a strong first impression, and the recruiter will be rooting for you the rest of the interview. If you bomb it, the recruiter may rule you out before you get to the next question.

In Chapter 5, I'll explain how to answer this question as well as other opening questions using a technique called the P-E-N framework. This framework can be extremely powerful for organizing your answers in clear, compelling ways.

Here are a few examples of opening questions, which we'll cover in Chapter 5:
- Tell me about yourself.
- Walk me through your resume.
- Why are you interested in this job?

Fit Questions: The second type of question is called a fit question. Recruiters may ask you a fit question to see if you'll be a good fit for their organization. A common example is "what's your greatest strength?" Your answers will tell recruiters a lot about your personality and how well you might integrate into their company culture.

In Chapter 6, I'll explain how to use the S-T-A-R framework to answer fit questions. When used effectively, this framework can help you impress recruiters with your communication skills and ability to get results.

Here are examples of fit questions that we'll cover in Chapter 6:
- What is your greatest strength or weakness?
- Tell me about a time when you've demonstrated analytical skills.
- Tell me about your leadership style.

Case Questions: The third type of question is called a case question. With case questions, recruiters ask you to explain how you'd handle specific job situations. With this type of question, they'll be testing your knowledge and your ability to exercise good judgment in a work situation.

Since most case questions are specific to particular career fields, you should see if you can find a list of case questions for your major. In Chapter 7, I'll explain how to answer case questions for career fields including business, healthcare, engineering, and computer science. If you're in a different field, you may want to get advice for answering industry-specific case questions from a professor, a career counselor, or someone else in your academic area.

Here are few common case questions:
- Business: "If your company's sales were declining, what would you do?"

- Healthcare: "If a patient faints in front of you, what would you do?"
- Engineering: "If I asked you to design a new highway intersection, how would you approach that?"
- Education: "If a child was being disruptive in your class, what would you do?"

Let's see how the characters in our story go about getting their lists of interview questions.

* * *

Billy greeted Jim at their next weekly meeting and asked, "Did you update your resume?"

Jim handed Billy a sheet of paper. "Yep, here it is. What do you think?"

Billy scanned the page. "Nice. It's easy to read. Your bullet points are strong. It's so much better than what you showed me last week."

Jim smiled. "So I passed?"

"Yeah. You're ready to move on to the next step. Now we're gonna work on your interview skills." Billy handed Jim two pieces of paper. "Here are two lists of

4. YOUR LIST OF INTERVIEW QUESTIONS

interview questions. The first page includes opening questions, which are the questions that recruiters typically ask at the beginning of interviews."

Jim looked at the page, and he saw a list that included "tell me about yourself, walk me through your resume," and about a dozen other questions.

Billy continued, "The second page includes fit questions. With these questions, recruiters are trying to figure out if you'll be a good fit for their companies." On that page, Jim saw "what's your greatest strength, what's your leadership style," and about twenty other questions.

"This seems like a lot of questions," Jim said.

"That's not all of them," Billy replied. "We haven't even gotten to the case questions yet."

Jim cringed. "How many of these questions am I gonna need?"

"Probably forty or fifty. But don't worry. You'll only need about a dozen answers. I'll show you how to use a few answers for a variety of questions. Now I'll see if I can find some case questions for your major." Billy started typing on his laptop. "Let's see … lawyer, librarian, management consultant, math teacher. It looks like I don't have any case questions for marketers."

"What's a case question?"

"It's a question that's specific to a particular career field. Recruiters ask them to see if you know your stuff."

"Well, if you don't have a list of case questions, where can I get one?"

"I bet your marketing club has a list. Are you a member?"

"I guess. I went to a few meetings last year, so I think that makes me a member. My friend Emily is an officer. I'll see if she has any case questions. While I'm here, do you have any questions for nursing, engineering, or computer science?"

Billy tilted his head. "Why? Are you planning to quadruple major?"

"No. The other people in my interview group might want questions for their majors."

Billy scanned though the folders on his computer. "Here's a list for nursing, and another one for engineering. I can't find anything for computer science."

"OK, I'll take what you've got."

Billy emailed the questions to Jim and said goodbye.

Jim sent a text to Emily asking for a list of marketing case questions. Within a few hours, she responded to him with an email. When Jim opened the attachment, he found a list of thirty case questions including the following:

4. YOUR LIST OF INTERVIEW QUESTIONS

- You just launched a new advertising campaign, and your sales start going down. What do you do?
- What is your favorite marketing campaign, and why?

At his next interview group meeting, Jim told his fellow group members, "Good news. I've got a bunch of interview questions for us to start practicing with."

He explained what he had learned about opening questions, fit questions, and case questions. He emailed the lists of questions to his fellow group members. As they looked through the lists, Jim explained how they could get additional questions from student organizations and online job sites. After a brief discussion, the group members decided to spend a few more days building their lists of questions so they could start practicing their answers the following week.

At their next meeting, they built a combined list of their top opening and fit questions. They also each built separate lists of case questions for their specific career fields. Those lists would guide them through the next few weeks of interview practice.

***

Now that each of our characters has a good list of interview questions, it's time for you to find your own list to practice with.

Getting a list of interview questions should be the easiest part of the job hunting process. Since most recruiters ask similar questions, it's easy to find a list of commonly asked questions.

On my website, I've included a list of questions you can use as a starting point. Then, you can add to that list with questions you find during the research you do yourself. Just go to AmazingJobSkills.com and click on the "Templates" link that's in the menu at the top of the page. You'll find a list of interview questions to get you started.

In the next three chapters, I've included suggestions and frameworks to help you answer a variety of interview questions. I've also included sample answers to common questions so you can hear what really good answers sound like.

See page 159 for a list of interview questions to get your started.

5. OPENING QUESTIONS

5. Opening Questions

Recruiters often start interviews with a few opening questions to help them decide if you have the basic skills needed to do the job. With these questions, you can set the tone for the interview and distinguish yourself from other candidates.

As I mentioned in the previous chapter, the most important question is typically "tell me about yourself" or "walk me through your resume." Your answer can be the same regardless of which version of this question recruiters ask you. You should keep practicing and refining your answer until you have a response that will absolutely dazzle them.

First impressions are incredibly powerful, so developing winning answers to opening questions should be the most important part of your interview preparation. Your answers should be fairly brief, lasting less than two minutes. Include highlights from your life, but don't go into detail about any specific experiences. You want to give an overview of your background, not an in-depth story about any particular experience.

I recommend you use the P-E-N framework for these questions. P-E-N stands for passion, experience, and next.

Your well-practiced answer using this framework will show that you're a better choice than other candidates who might give unstructured answers or irrelevant details about themselves.

P is for PASSION:

Start by telling the recruiter what you're passionate about. Make sure you choose a passion that's related to the job you want. Recruiters are looking for people who will enjoy their work, so let them know what you enjoy.

For example, someone in the accounting field might say, "I'm an organizer. I really enjoy organizing things into neat, orderly groups." Someone applying for a consulting job might say, "I love strategy. I enjoy defining clear objectives and identifying the best options to meet those objectives."

Now, go back to the job descriptions for your targeted companies and figure out what passions you have that relate to the duties for those jobs.

E is for EXPERIENCE:

Summarize your experiences that are relevant for the job you want. You should do this briefly without going into too much detail. This will give the interviewer context for the rest of the interview.

Our aspiring accountant might say, "I'm the treasurer for my school's accounting club. In that role, I've put in place a new bookkeeping system that makes it easier for us to see where we're spending our money." Our consultant could say, "My interest in strategy helped me win my high school's chess competition. Chess is all about knowing which options are best to accomplish your objective. Identifying those options and prioritizing them is something I'm especially good at."

Look over your resume and think about your work experiences that are most relevant for the job you want. Then, practice summarizing those experiences into a few sentences.

N is for NEXT:

Tell the interviewer the type of experience you'd like to get next. Your answer should be directly related to the role they're trying to fill. Here are examples for the N section of the P-E-N framework:

Our accounting student might say, "Next, I'm looking for a summer job where I can apply my passion for organizing things. I'd like to work for your accounting firm

5. OPENING QUESTIONS

where I can build my skills in bookkeeping, auditing, and tax accounting." Our consulting student could end with, "Next, I want to find a summer job that will help me accomplish my goal of becoming a business consultant. I've researched my options, and I believe your company is the best fit for my skills and interests. Hopefully, you'll see that I'm a great fit for what you're looking for."

Let's see how the characters in our story use the P-E-N framework to answer opening questions.

* * *

When Jim stopped at the career development office for his next weekly meeting, Billy greeted him. "Hey Jim, are you ready for your first mock interview?"

"I guess. Where do we start?"

Billy smiled. "We start where interviews usually start: tell me about yourself."

"That's easy. I was born in South Carolina, about a hundred miles from here. I moved to Charleston when I was ten years old, and I started running track which has taught me a lot about hard work. Now I'm studying marketing, running track, and I'm a member of the debate team. Doing all those activities is teaching me time management skills. How was that?"

Billy gave Jim a stern look. "Honestly, it was bad ... really bad. I wouldn't hire you after that."

Jim looked confused. "Why? I told you about myself. Isn't that what you wanted?"

"Yeah, but what you said wasn't relevant for a marketing job. It didn't make me want to hire you."

"OK, so what should I say?"

"Let's start with the job description. What do marketers do?"

Jim reached into his backpack and pulled out a binder. In it, he found the job description for his targeted job, and he read from it. "Marketers analyze information, develop marketing campaigns, and lead teams of subject matter experts."

"Great," said Billy. "Have you ever done any of those things?"

"Yeah, but shouldn't I wait until I get asked about my work experiences before talking about them?"

"Absolutely not. You should mention your most relevant experiences in your opening. Just don't go into too much detail. Let's try it again. Tell me about yourself, and

5. OPENING QUESTIONS

this time, tell me what you've done that'll make you a good marketer."

"OK. I'm studying marketing, and I've gotten really good at analyzing information, developing marketing materials, and leading teams. How's that?"

Billy made a yawning motion as he covered his mouth. "Yawn. You're killing me. You've got to tell me something interesting."

Jim was getting frustrated. "I don't get it. I'm telling you about myself. I'm telling you the skills I have. What do you want?"

"Let me show you how it's done." Billy cleared his throat. "My name is Billy Jackson, and I have a passion for working with kids. As you can see from my resume, I spent two summers as a camp counselor. During that time, I worked with over a hundred kids who were between the ages of ten and thirteen. My favorite part of that job was helping them improve their skills. My specialty was taking complicated tasks, like setting up overnight campsites, and breaking those tasks into easy-to-understand steps.

"When I was hired to come back for my second summer, I was promoted to Senior Camp Counselor. I was given more responsibility and larger class sizes. In addition to teaching survival skills, I became the lead instructor for our camp's writing and crafts classes. I also coached several sports including basketball and soccer.

"As I said, I love working with kids, especially kids between the ages of ten and thirteen. I'm looking to start my career as a middle school teaching assistant or substitute teacher. I'd like to find a position in a school district where I can build my skills and eventually become a full-time teacher. I'm hoping it will be with your school district."

Jim looked stunned. "Wow. I'd hire you today. How did you do that?"

Billy smiled. "Let me break it down for you. I use something called the P-E-N framework. The P is for passion. I start by telling the recruiter what I'm passionate about. For a teaching career, a good choice is a passion for working with kids. You'll have to figure out what your passion is that relates to marketing.

"The E is for experience. I give a brief summary of the experience I have that's related to the job I want. Since they're hiring teachers, I tell them about my relevant teaching experience.

"The N is for next. I tell them what I want to do next. This one's easy. My next is exactly the same as the job they are hiring for."

5. OPENING QUESTIONS

Jim was taking notes. "Let's see if I have this right. My P should be my passion, and it should be something that'll make me good at the job. E is the experience I have related to that job. N is what I want to do next, and it should be the same as the job I'm interviewing for. Is that right?"

Billy nodded. "Yep. Now go practice your answer using the P-E-N framework."

"OK. What else should I do this week?"

"That's plenty. Getting your opening answer right is the most important part of the interview. You'll need this entire week to get a good answer. When you come back next week, I want you to blow me away when I ask you to tell me about yourself."

Jim thanked Billy and left for his interview group meeting. He arrived at the student lounge about an hour before his other group members were scheduled to get there. He sat at an empty table and reached into his backpack. He pulled out his resume, the job description for his targeted job, and his laptop.

On his laptop, he typed PASSION at the top of a blank page. Then he typed several options including figuring out what motivates people, creating marketing campaigns, and leading big projects. Next, he typed

EXPERIENCE. Under that heading, he entered examples of his work experience from his resume. Finally, he typed NEXT and a few bullet points that described his dream job.

After Jim had been sitting there for about an hour, Sarah, Abby, and Ethan walked up together. As they sat down, Abby said, "Hey Jim, are you ready to get started?"

Jim smiled. "You bet. Who wants to ask me the first interview question?"

Sarah opened her laptop to find her list of interview questions. "I'll do it. Jim, tell me about yourself."

"OK. My name is Jim Harrison, and I've always been passionate about figuring out what motivates people. For the past two summers, I've been working as a camp counselor, which has given me great opportunities to observe and influence people. During my first summer there, I volunteered to redesign our camp's website. I interviewed kids and parents to see what motivated them to choose our camp, and based on my findings, I built a website that helped generate a 30% increase in applications.

"The next summer, I was promoted to the position of Camp Communications Manager. I loved that job because it gave me additional opportunities to figure out what motivated parents and kids to choose specific summer camps. I conducted research and built a marketing strategy that's projected to increase applications by another 40%.

"Next, I'm looking for a position where I can use my passion for motivating people to build compelling marketing campaigns. I want a role where I can analyze information and identify business opportunities. I'd also like a role where I can work with diverse cross-functional teams and agency partners. I'm hoping it will be with your company.

"How was that?"

Sarah, Abby, and Ethan just stared at him for a few seconds. Finally, Sarah broke the silence. "Jim, I gotta tell you, I'm blown away. If I was a recruiter, I'd give you a job. How'd you do that?"

Jim smiled. He explained the P-E-N framework. They all agreed to use the framework to build their own answer to the "tell me about yourself" question. At the next group meeting, they'd practice their answers with each other.

A few days later, the group met back at the student lounge. Ethan started by saying, "Abby, are you ready to tell us about yourself?"

Abby smiled. "I'm ready. My name is Abby Walker, and I've always been passionate about solving complicated problems. From the time I was a kid, I've looked for problems that other people found difficult, and I've challenged myself to solve them.

"I applied that passion during my high school science fair competition where I won first place in the engineering category. My project was titled 'Stronger Construction Designs for Bridges,' and it addressed a complicated challenge that engineers have been working on for centuries.

"I chose engineering as my college major because of my interest in solving complicated problems. As you can see on my resume, I have experience in everything from developing improvements for construction techniques to creating engineering plans for dog kennels. I'm also the treasure for our university's physics club, which has helped me build finance-related skills, and I'm a staff reporter for our school's newspaper, which helps me polish my writing skills.

"I'm looking for a position where I can apply my passion for solving problems to more advanced challenges. I hope to get a job where I can develop engineering plans, prepare budgets, and write reports. I hope that job is with your company."

5. OPENING QUESTIONS

Ethan clapped his hands together. "That was awesome. You're a rock star." Jim and Sarah agreed. They each gave Abby a few suggestions. Then, they turned their attention to Ethan.

Ethan grinned. "Listen and learn. My name is Ethan Wright, and I'm passionate about computers. I've always been good at anything related to computers. Whether it's building new software applications or setting up networks, I'm your guy.

"For the past few summers, I've worked at my family's computer store. That's involved installing hardware and software, and I'm a good at debugging computer issues. I'm getting my degree in computer science, and last year, I won our computer club's annual programming competition.

"I'd like to find a job where I can trouble-shoot computer problems full-time. I'd like it to be with a company that's nearby so I can stay close to my family."

Ethan leaned back in his chair and smiled. "Nailed it!"

Jim, Sarah, and Abby looked at each other. Jim spoke first. "I think you have a good start, and I like your choice for your passion. What surprised me is that you focused on the technical aspect of computers. You're a people-person, and you didn't talk about that at all. Don't you think you should talk about your ability to work well with others?"

"I know I like working with people," Ethan replied, "but I'm applying for a computer job, not a people job."

"I don't know," said Abby. "I think what sets you apart is that you've got a good balance of computer skills and people skills. You should play that up in your answer. Tell them that you can address computer issues AND work well with others. Also, your answer was really short. Maybe you should add something about your Eagle Scout project. That would be interesting, and it seems relevant."

Jim added, "One more thing ... you mentioned your family's computer store and how important family is to you. I wouldn't talk about your family in an interview. If I were a recruiter, I'd worry that you just want a job at my company to get some quick experience, and you'll leave to work at your family's business."

Ethan looked at Jim and said, "That's exactly what I don't want to do. I'm trying to get out of my family's business."

Jim nodded. "Then don't bring up your family. Just tell them about your experience and that you want to get a great job where you can pursue your passion."

5. OPENING QUESTIONS

Ethan typed a few notes into his computer, then turned to Sarah. "Sarah, you're up. Tell us about yourself."

Sarah looked nervous. "OK. My name is Sarah Barker. I'm getting a dual degree in nursing and psychology. I'm from Wisconsin, and I really like being here in South Carolina where the weather's warmer.

"I moved to University City because I heard the nursing program at Southern State is outstanding, and I've really enjoyed the people I've met here. The classes have been great too.

"Shortly after I got here, I joined the university's healthcare club, and my fellow students elected me vice president. I'm hoping to use that role to improve the resources our club has for students. Is there anything else you'd like to know about me?"

When Sarah finished, there was an uncomfortable silence. Finally, Ethan broke the silence. "Girl, you're all over the place. What happened to your P-E-N framework?"

"Sorry," Sarah responded. "I got nervous, and I forgot what I wanted to say."

Abby put her hand gently on Sarah's shoulder. "Don't worry. That's why we're here. Let's go through this together. Tell us why you chose your majors."

Sarah thought for a moment. "I just like helping people."

Abby smiled. "Good. We can work with that. Try starting with 'I have a passion for helping people.' Then explain what you've done about that. Didn't you tell us that you volunteered for a charity when you were in high school?"

"Yeah, but I feel bad using a charity to get a job."

Ethan said, "Come on. It's not using the charity. It's telling the story of your life. Here. Give me your resume."

Sarah handed her resume to Ethan.

Ethan scanned it. "You've got all kinds of great stuff in here about helping people. I mean you're like a regular Mother Teresa."

For the next hour, the group helped Sarah build her answer to the "tell me about yourself" question. Finally, she was ready to try it again.

"My name is Sarah Barker, and I've always had a passion for helping people. When I was in high school, I volunteered for a charity called Hearts for Children. That's where I first spent time with nurses and psychologists. I really admired the way they helped kids who were dealing with chronic diseases.

"I've had two summer jobs that I've absolutely loved. The first was as an orderly at a retirement home. I did everything from feeding patients to helping them get around the facilities. I was honored to receive their Employee of the Month award because the patients and family members rated me so high on surveys they filled out.

"My other summer job was as a nursing assistant at a big medical center. My job was to help nurses take vitals and record medical histories. I also learned to use a new software program they were installing, and I trained fifteen of their nurses on the program. I'm good with computers, and I loved showing people how to use software that they weren't familiar with.

"I know how stressful it is for patients and their family members when they're dealing with medical problems, so in addition to getting a nursing degree, I'm getting a degree in psychology. I hope that will give me a better understanding of how people think and what I can do to help them get through tough times.

"I'm looking for a position where I can help people when they're being treated at medical facilities. Based on my research, I think your organization will be a great place for me to do that."

Again, the group was silent. Jim finally said, "That was great. I'm trying to think of things you can do to improve it, but I'm at a loss." Abby and Ethan nodded their heads in agreement.

The group decided to call it a day and practice their answers again at their next meeting. When they reconvened, they each recited their responses to "tell me about yourself" one more time. Then they moved on to other opening questions including "walk me through your resume" and "why are you a good choice for this job?"

After a few more days of practice, they agreed to move on to fit questions.

* * *

As you can see from this story, it's much easier to answer opening questions when you have a good framework. I recommend you use the P-E-N framework so recruiters can find out what you're passionate about, what relevant experience you have, and what you want to do next.

When recruiters ask you to tell them about yourself, you may think they want to hear about your personal life. They really don't. They want to hear why you'll be a good choice for the job they have to offer. Limit your answers to information that directly relates to the job unless they say they want to hear about something else.

Here are some dos and don'ts for opening questions:

Dos:

- Limit your answers to two minutes or less. Your answers should be long enough to get the interviewer interested in you, but not so long that you're monopolizing the conversation.
- Start with your passion, and make sure it's relevant for the job you want. Then, briefly summarize your work experience. This should be done in five to ten sentences. You'll have time to go into more detail later in the interview. Finally, finish with what you want to do next, which is work in the type of job that the recruiter is interviewing you for.
- As you talk about your experience, mention your biggest accomplishments, any promotions you've received, and any major awards you've won.

Don'ts:
- Don't include personal information, such as details about your family, friends, or hobbies that are unrelated to the job. Recruiters want to know why you would make a good employee. They really don't want to know about your personal details.
- Don't be negative about anything. No matter how bad your previous jobs or bosses were, don't ever say anything negative about them during an interview. Recruiters want to hire positive people, so show them how positive you can be.
- Don't go into too much detail on any specific topic. The recruiters want to see that you can summarize information without getting caught up in details. Just give them high-level answers here, then go into the details later in the interview.

Now that you know how to approach opening questions, practice these questions with your interview group members. Then, you'll be ready to move onto the next type of questions.

5. OPENING QUESTIONS

See page 163 for templates and examples to help you practice for opening questions.

6. Fit Questions

Recruiters might ask fit questions to see if you'd be a good fit for their company. Typically, these questions start with "tell me about a time when..." or "how would you handle a situation if..." Recruiters want to see if your answers would be appropriate for their company and the role they're trying to fill.

Here are a few popular fit questions you might hear during an interview:

- Tell me about a time when you demonstrated leadership.
- How would you handle a situation if you had to deal with a difficult person on a project?
- Have you ever developed a creative solution to a challenging problem?
- What's your greatest strength?
- What's your biggest weakness?

For these questions, I recommend you use something called the S-T-A-R framework, which stands for situation, task, actions, and result. It's the easiest way to structure clear, compelling responses. Here's how it works:

S is for SITUATION:

Start with one sentence that describes the situation you were in. This could be as simple as saying where you were working and what your job title was.

T is for TASK:

In one sentence, tell the interviewer what your assignment was. This could be a task assigned to you by an employer, a teacher, or a peer.

A is for ACTIONS:

In a few sentences, explain the actions you took to complete your task. Don't talk about what a group of people did. Recruiters want to hear about the actions you took, so make it clear what you specifically did.

R is for RESULT:

Tell the recruiter about the result from your actions. If possible, quantify those results or explain how you delivered something above and beyond what the task called for.

Here's an example that shows how a graphic artist might use the S-T-A-R framework to answer a fit question like "tell me about a time when you solved a problem with a creative approach."

Situation: "I was a freelance designer working on a project for a local smoothie shop."

Task: "My client wanted me to redesign their online menu."

Actions: "I spent an afternoon at the smoothie shop, and I asked customers what they liked most about the place. They told me they liked the cheerful atmosphere and fresh fruits that were used in the smoothies. Since that's what customers liked most, I designed the new online menu with bright, cheerful colors, and I included images of fresh fruits on it."

Result: "Since the smoothie shop switched from their text-based online menu to my design with the bright colors and images of fresh fruits, their online orders have doubled."

Here's another example that shows how a sales person might use the S-T-A-R approach to answer a question like "tell me about a time when you used your persuasion skills."

Situation: "I was working at the Eastern University bookstore as a sales representative."

Task: "My manager asked me to persuade the business school professors to recommend our store to their students."

Actions: "I hosted a free lunch for the professors, and I asked them questions during that event. They told me they were frustrated because their students might remember to buy textbooks, but they'd forget to buy workbooks. I told the professors that my bookstore would bundle all the books for each class together so students would automatically get every book they needed including the workbooks they might have forgotten otherwise. Then, I asked the professors to recommend my bookstore to their students."

Result: "The next semester, our sales of business books went up 30% because the professors told their students to get all the books they needed from our store."

For these types of questions, you should have five or six stories prepared. With the right stories, you can cover a broad range of questions. For example, you should have stories that can flex to address the following topics:

- Leadership which includes building a team and getting results
- Creativity which involves finding innovative solutions to challenging problems

- Collaboration which could include building relationships and demonstrating interpersonal skills
- Persistence which means working through difficult situations

You should prepare a few different stories for these topics, and you should be ready to adapt your stories to answer any fit question a recruiter might ask.

Let's see how the characters in our story approach fit questions.

* * *

At their next weekly meeting, Billy told Jim that they were going to have a walk-and-talk. Jim was surprised. "What's a walk-and-talk?"

Billy put on his jacket. "It means we're gonna walk around and talk as we go. Sometimes it helps to get a change in scenery."

Jim followed Billy out of the career development office. "Sounds good to me."

6. FIT QUESTIONS

As they walked across the campus, Billy asked Jim how his response to "tell me about yourself" was coming along. Jim shared his version of his P-E-N answer.

"That's great. Keep working on it so it's even stronger, and make minor changes based on the details of the jobs you're interviewing for. Let's move on to fit questions."

"Tell me again, which ones are fit questions?"

"They're the kind recruiters ask to see if you're a good fit for their organization. Fit questions can include anything from 'what's your greatest strength' to 'tell me about a time when you demonstrated leadership.'

"With fit questions, it's best to give examples of what you've done that shows you have the skills they're asking about. I'm gonna tell you how to use the S-T-A-R framework to answers these questions."

"I thought the best approach to use was the P-E-N framework."

"That's for opening questions. For fit questions, you should use the S-T-A-R framework. Start with the situation you were in. For example, you could say that you were working as a camp counselor.

"Then, tell them what your task was. That's the T in the S-T-A-R. Your task might have been to teach kids to set up a campsite.

"The A in S-T-A-R is for actions. You should tell them the actions you took to accomplish your task. That could include what you did to get kids to build the campsite.

"Finally, tell them the result you got. Try to make it as measurable as possible. Recruiters love results with numbers, so try to find stories where your results can be quantified."

Jim said, "I think I get it, but can you give me an example?"

Billy smiled. "Here's my S-T-A-R story when I get the question 'tell me about a time when you demonstrated creativity.' I was working as a camp counselor. My task was to get a group of teenage boys to send messages home. In previous years, that meant they'd have to write letters to their parents.

"First, I asked the boys to tell me how they liked to communicate with their friends when they weren't together. They mentioned recording short videos that they'd send to each other. Next, I asked what they wanted their parents to know about the camp. They talked about the sports they played and the friends they spent time with. Then, we all recorded short videos that showed us playing sports and hanging out with friends. Those are the actions I took.

"The result of this creative exercise was that I took an assignment that most of the boys were dreading, and I found a way to make it interesting for them. In our end-of-summer survey, most of the boys rated the video production as their favorite activity of the entire summer. Their parents also rated the video as their favorite communication that they received from our camp. That was my result. So there you have it, my S-T-A-R answer that includes the situation, task, actions, and result."

Jim stopped walking and turned to Billy. "So, let's see if I've got this right. Start with the situation, which is the job I was in. Then, describe my task, which is the assignment I was trying to accomplish. Next, tell the actions I took, and finish with the result I got. I like that. How many of those S-T-A-R stories will I need?"

"I recommend you take your top five or six experiences and turn them into S-T-A-R stories. Let's look through your resume and pick out a few things that might make good stories."

They sat on a nearby bench and Jim pulled his resume out of his backpack. As they looked at it together, Billy asked, "What's been your biggest accomplishment?"

Jim thought about it. "I think it would be the marketing strategy I built for our camp."

"Great. For your homework assignment, I want you to write down one sentence that describes the situation and another sentence for your task. Then, write down a few specific actions you took and the result you got."

Jim looked puzzled. "Which question will my story have to answer?"

Billy said, "That story could work for a variety of questions. It could answer how you demonstrated creativity or how you found a solution to a challenging problem. If you worked with anyone else on that project, it could also answer how you demonstrated leadership or collaboration."

"So I can use one story to answer different questions?"

"Absolutely. In a story like that, you probably had to be creative, maybe analytical, and maybe even a good leader. Just change up the wording in your answer to focus on whatever skill the recruiter's asking you about."

6. FIT QUESTIONS

Jim and Billy identified a few other experiences Jim could use to build more S-T-A-R answers to interview questions, and they walked back to the career development office. When they got there, Jim thanked Billy and went to the student lounge.

Jim saw Sarah sitting by herself at a table, and he walked over to her. "Hey, Sarah. Can I join you?"

"Sure. I'm just killing time until our meeting. Did you get any good tips from your interview guru?"

"Yep, Billy was a wealth of information today." Jim explained the S-T-A-R framework to Sarah, and he told her about his homework assignment. "I need to write my S-T-A-R stories for four or five things I've done. Do you think you could help me?"

They spent the next hour working on Jim's S-T-A-R stories, and by the time Abby and Ethan joined them, Jim had four examples to share with them.

"Alright team, before we move on to fit questions, let's do one quick round of our 'tell me about yourself' answers. Abby started, followed by Ethan, Jim, and Sarah. When they each finished, they agreed that their answers were amazing, and they were ready to tackle that question in interviews.

Jim transitioned the group to their next task. "We've graduated from the opening questions to the fit questions. Those are the ones that help recruiters decide if we're a good fit for their companies." Jim pulled out his list of questions and read a few of the fit questions to the group. Then he explained the S-T-A-R framework and gave an example of his best S-T-A-R story. The others pulled out their resumes and started looking for experiences they could use for their S-T-A-R stories.

At the end of their time together that day, they agree to spend the next few meetings asking each other fit questions and practicing their answers. After they adjourned, Jim and Sarah walked out of the student lounge together. As they left the building, Jim said, "Emily asked me to show you around campus. Are you interested in me giving you a tour sometime?"

With a smile, Sarah said, "OK. How long until your next class?"

"I've got about two hours," Jim lied. His next class started in fifteen minutes, but he didn't want to pass up this chance to spend more time with Sarah. For the next two hours, they walked around the campus and shared stories about their lives. Jim escorted Sarah to her dorm where they said goodbye, then he sprinted to the business

6. FIT QUESTIONS

school. It was the first time he skipped a class, and he wanted to find one of his classmates to see what he missed.

At their next meeting, the group split into pairs to practice their S-T-A-R stories. Jim and Ethan went to one table; Sarah and Abby went to another. When the guys sat down, Ethan smiled. "So, Jimbo, what's going on with you and Sarah?"

Jim pretended not to know what Ethan was talking about. "What do ya mean?"

"I saw you walking with her out of the lounge. Then, I passed you walking with her around campus. Are you two a thing?"

"A thing? Nah, I'm just being a good school ambassador. She's new to campus, so I gave her a tour."

Ethan grinned. "I'm on to you. I see the way you look at her."

Jim shrugged it off. "We're here to practice interviewing, so let's get to it. Here's your first question. Tell me about a time when you said something that didn't annoy other people?"

Ethan laughed. "Alright, I'll leave you alone … for now. Ask me a real interview question."

"OK. What's your biggest strength?"

"I'd say it's my ability to annoy other people."

"Come on, Ethan. Get serious. I don't have all day."

"Fine. I'd say my biggest strength is my ability to diagnose problems. I'll give you an example from when I was working as a computer technician at an electronics store. My task was to figure out why a customer's network kept going down. The customer thought it was because we sold him defective equipment, and he wanted a refund for $50,000 worth of computers he had purchased from our store.

"First, I asked the customer a series of questions about the issue. He said his network kept crashing around noon on weekdays, and his in-house technicians couldn't figure out why. I went to his office and observed people using the computers. Around noon every day, his employees took their lunch breaks. I noticed many of them were playing games on their computers, which was allowed as long as it only happened during their breaks. The issue was that the network couldn't handle the high-bandwidth games that the employees were playing. The next day, I installed a $100 router that was able to handle the surge in bandwidth, and that solved the issue of the network crashing.

"Because I'm good at asking the right questions and observing what's happening, I was able to diagnose a

6. FIT QUESTIONS

problem that other technicians couldn't. As a result, I was able to save my employer $50,000 in refund costs. In the end, all it took was a $100 router that I installed myself. Since then, that customer has purchased another $50,000 in equipment because he was so happy with the service I provided.

"How's that?"

Jim pursed his lips. "I have to admit, that was good. I like the way you gave an example with the situation, task, actions, and result. Nicely done. Now my turn. Ask me anything."

Ethan smiled. "OK. Are you interested in Sarah?"

Jim sighed. "Let me be more specific. Ask me a fit interview question."

"Fine. Tell me about a time when you demonstrated an ability to find a solution to a challenging problem."

"Good. I like that one. The situation happened when I was working as a counselor at the Hillside Explorers Camp. The camp's general manager told me we didn't get enough applications to fill all the slots we had available for students, and she didn't know why more families weren't applying for our camp. Because we weren't filling all our slots, she thought she might have to hire fewer counselors the next summer. I got her approval to look into why we weren't getting more applications.

"I started by emailing people who had sent their kids to our camp in previous years but not that year. I wanted to find out why they stopped sending their kids to our camp. Some of them responded and said their kids liked activities that other camps were offering. I then researched other camps, and I found some activities they offered that we didn't. I then surveyed the families on our mailing list, and from those survey results, I identified three new activities that both kids and parents wanted. Next, I got our general manager's approval to launch those three activities and create a marketing campaign to tell prospective families about them.

"I was able to solve this challenging problem by investigating what prospective customers wanted and developing solutions for them. The result was that I created three new activities and a marketing campaign that led to a 30% increase in applications the following year. I'm especially happy because those new activities were some of the most popular ones among students the next summer.

"How's that?"

Ethan nodded. "Nice. Very good."

6. FIT QUESTIONS

Jim and Ethan practiced a few more questions. Then they regrouped with Sarah and Abby to discuss their game plan. Together, they all agreed to spend their next meeting polishing their answers to a variety of fit questions.

Two days later, Jim started their meeting by saying, "Is everyone ready for a round of fit questions?"

The other group members gave an enthusiastic "yes."

Jim continued with, "Let's each answer one more fit question before we move on to the next category."

Ethan responded. "OK, Jim. Let's start with you. What's your biggest strength?"

Jim nodded. "My biggest strength is my ability to identify opportunities that other people might miss. Let me give you an example from when I volunteered to be the webmaster for our university's running club. My task was to use our website to increase participation at our monthly fun runs.

"First, I did some research and learned that most students weren't even aware that we had a running club on campus. While our awareness was below 5%, I learned that nearly 25% of students would be interested in coming to our runs if they knew about 'em ahead of time. I also found out the university would publicize events on their social media sites free of charge for any student organization. Next, I created social media posts for our running club on Facebook, Instagram, and Twitter. These posts provided the information students wanted about the locations, dates, and times for each run. Then, I posted weekly articles about the upcoming fun runs on our university's social media feeds. Those articles drove traffic to our websites where students could sign up for our races.

"The result was a 300% increase in participation for our fun runs. I was able to get that result because I looked beyond our club's website and found opportunities to use social media to get more people to our events."

Ethan smiled. "Nice. You did a great job explaining the situation and your task. Your actions were clear, and your results were strong. Well done." Ethan turned to Sarah and Abby. "Ladies, anything to add?"

They shook her heads. Abby replied, "Not for Jim. Let's give you a try. Ethan, tell me about a time when you demonstrated analytical skills."

Ethan paused for a second. "OK. When I was in high school, I was working to get my Eagle Scout certification. For my final project, I decided to design a new computer network for my high school. I chose that project because of my passion for computers and because our school's network was frequently going down.

"I started by calculating the data usage for the network. I learned that our usage was 50% higher than other high school of similar size and that our usage was doubling every year. Then, I projected the bandwidth needs for the next five years and determined how much the network would need to expand over time. I used that information to design a network that could handle the current usage requirements and be expandable to handle future needs. Since we only needed the bandwidth from 8:00 a.m. to 5:00 p.m. on weekdays, I researched other places that could use our network during our downtimes. I found a nearby university that was willing to buy our available bandwidth on evenings and weekends.

"As a result, I designed and installed a new network that reduced downtime by 97% over the next three years. Plus, that network cost 40% less than the network our school district's IT department originally recommended.

"How's that?"

Abby replied, "Very good?" She turned to Sarah. "Your turn. What's your biggest weakness?"

Sarah frowned. "That's a tough one." She paused, then said, "I'd say my biggest weakness has been my hesitancy to be assertive. I have a diplomatic style, and I'm working on being more assertive when needed. Let me give you an example from when I was an orderly at the Pleasanton Retirement Home. One of my tasks was to transition patients from a common area to their rooms at the end of each day.

"One time, there was an elderly woman who wasn't willing to leave the common area. I tried every diplomatic approach I could think of to coax her to her room. Nothing worked. Finally, another orderly came in and firmly told the woman that she had to go to her room or she'd lose the privilege of coming to the common area the next day. I originally thought that threatening a resident like that might seem rude, but it worked in that situation.

"As a result, I've learned to be more assertive when needed. I still start with a diplomatic approach, but I'm more willing to become assertive if the situation calls for it."

Ethan responded, "That's a good answer. Since nurses have to be diplomatic, I like the way your weakness isn't a deal-breaker for your career. I also like the way you explain what you're doing to overcome that weakness."

"Thanks," replied Sarah. "Now it's Abby's turn. Abby, tell me about a time you demonstrated creativity."

Abby responded, "Last summer, I was an assistant office manager at an animal shelter. My task was to find a way to increase the number of dogs we could keep in our kennel building.

"I started by researching places where populations were becoming more dense. I noticed that in cities, many people lived in high-rise buildings, and they often lived with multiple people in small apartments. I decided to apply those lessons to our dog kennels. I designed kennels that could be stacked on top of each other so we could fit more kennels in the same space. I also researched which dog breeds and genders were most likely to coexist peacefully in the same living space. I built prototype kennel-apartments and tested them with a variety of dogs. After weeks of testing, I made adjustments to the designs, and I supervised a contractor who converted all our small-dog kennels to my new apartment-style design.

"Because I found a creative solution, the result was a 40% increase in the number of dogs that could be housed in our kennel building. As an added benefit, I discovered that the dogs that moved in with roommates were less aggressive and more playful. We noticed that those dogs were 10% more likely to get adopted because their behavior appealed to people who came to our facility looking to find a pet."

Sarah smiled. "Wow, I like that example. It never would have occurred to me to use high-rise apartments as inspiration for designing dog kennels. Good job."

"Thanks," replied Abby.

The group practiced with a few more fit questions, then decided to move on to case questions in their next meeting.

* * *

As you can see from our story, fit questions can be challenging. With these types of questions, recruiters appreciate real-life stories. By telling stories about actions you've taken and results you've gotten, you'll give recruiters confidence that you have the experience needed to get things done.

One of my favorite sayings is "facts tell; stories sell." It means people often don't make decisions based on facts. You can tell a recruiter your grade point average, how many months of work experience you have, and how many classes you've taken in specific subjects. Those are facts, but they aren't very interesting.

6. FIT QUESTIONS

Recruiters are more impressed by stories about your experiences, especially if you include results you've gotten. That's why the S-T-A-R framework is so effective. It helps you frame up stories that have a beginning, a middle, and an end. In those stories, you are the hero. When you tell recruiters relevant stories about yourself, they'll remember you as the person who can do the types of things they want done.

Here are a few dos and don'ts for fit questions:

Dos:

- Have five or six stories ready to go. That way, you can answer a variety of fit questions.
- Use the S-T-A-R framework. Limit your S, T, and R to one or two sentences each. The recruiter wants to see that you can communicate succinctly, so spend your time on your actions, not the other aspects of your story.
- Be specific about your actions. Tell the recruiter exactly what you personally did.
- Make sure your results are clear and compelling. Always end your story with positive results. Recruiters are looking for problem solvers, so

compelling results are a must. If you didn't get a positive result, use a different story.

Don'ts:
- Don't ramble. Recruiters will lose interest if you take too long to get to the point.
- Don't say "we." Instead, say "I." Recruiters don't want to hear what a group of people did. They want to hear what you did. When you say "we," it's not clear what your role in the story is, so train yourself to always say "I" in your stories.

For reference, here's an example of how <u>not</u> to answer a fit question such as "tell me about a time when you demonstrated leadership."

"I've always been a great basketball player. In high school, I led my team in points per game and rebounds.

"I also once led a group of fellow Boy Scouts on a hike. We went to a beautiful national park, and I was the fastest hiker in the group. I was so fast that the other kids had difficulty keeping up with me.

"Another time, I led my school's debate team with the highest number of wins in our competitions. I'm very competitive, so I worked hard at beating my team members. If you hire me, I'll bring that competitive spirit, and I'll find a way to beat my co-workers at any goal you set for me."

First, this candidate gave too many examples, and each one was too brief to make a compelling point. A good answer to this question would focus on one example that included impressive results.

Also, this candidate doesn't seem to understand leadership. Rather than talking about being better than teammates, he should have focused on how he built a team that successfully accomplished a goal together. That way, the recruiter would see him as someone who could lead by motivating other people, not drive his coworkers crazy with his overly competitive nature.

See page 175 for templates and examples to help you practice for fit questions.

7. Case Questions

For case questions, recruiters might ask you to explain how you'd approach specific situations related to the job you want. They might ask you to explain how you'd address hypothetical situations like opportunities that arise in a business or emergencies that happen in a healthcare environment. They might also ask you to formulate a recommendation, assess a sample of someone's work, or make a persuasive argument.

Here are examples of case questions you might hear in interviews:

- Marketing: "What would you do if you needed to launch a new product?"
- Healthcare: "If you had a patient who was crashing, what would you do?"
- Engineering: "If I asked you to design a bridge that needed to last 1,000 years, how would do that?"
- Computer Science: "What questions would you ask if you needed to upgrade a computer network?"
- Education: "How would you handle a child who was being disruptive?"

7. CASE QUESTIONS

Recruiters typically ask case questions to test your problem-solving abilities or your knowledge about a specific subject. If you need a minute to gather your thoughts, I recommend you start your answer by asking a few clarifying questions. This will show that you can assess a situation before jumping to a conclusion. It will also buy you time to think of a good response.

You should also state your assumptions or your criteria for the answer you'll give. For example, if you're asked what your favorite medication is, you could start by saying that your answer would be based on criteria such as effectiveness in treating a medical condition and an absence of adverse side effects. This approach works well because it shows the recruiter that you can formulate recommendations based on relevant criteria. It also buys you a few extra seconds to think of a good response.

Let's see how the characters in our story address case questions.

* * *

When Jim arrived for their next weekly meeting, Billy introduced him to another career counselor. "Jim, this is Jamal. Today, you'll be meeting with him instead of me."

Jamal shook Jim's hand and said, "Nice to meet you."

Jim said hello, then turned to Billy. "What, are you tired of me already?"

Billy laughed. "Not at all. This week, you'll be working on case questions, and I won't be able to help you with that." Billy explained that case questions are specific to the career fields that people are in. "Marketing case questions are completely different from education case questions, so I'm having Jamal help you today. He's an expert on marketing questions."

Jim nodded. "Good. I just wanted to make sure you weren't firing me as your client."

Billy smiled. "You're not so lucky. You'll be back with me next week. I just need Jamal to impart his marketing wisdom on you today."

Jamal led Jim to a small conference room where they sat down. Once seated, Jamal asked, "Do you have your list of case questions?"

Jim pulled out the list he got from the marketing club. Jamal looked at it and said, "Good. This'll work." He then explained that most marketing case questions could be answered using two popular frameworks. "Have you learned the 3C's and the 4P's in your marketing classes yet?"

7. CASE QUESTIONS

Jim nodded. "Yep. If I remember right, the 3C's are customers, competitors, and company. I think the 4P's are product, price, promotion, and … and … and I don't remember the fourth P."

Jamal waited a moment to give Jim time to think. Finally, Jamal said, "place." He went on to explain how Jim could use those frameworks to answer most marketing case questions. "Let's say I wanted you to tell me what questions you'd ask if your brand's sales were declining. How would you answer that?"

Jim felt unsure. "Maybe I'd ask if I was advertising less?"

Jamal shook his head. "Not exactly. Listen to how I answer the question. First, I'd look at my customers. Are they buying from my category less often, or are their preferences changing so my products are less relevant for them? Next, I'd see what my competitors are doing. Have they launched any new products or marketing campaigns that might be impacting my sales, or have they reduced their prices on products that compete with mine? Finally, I'd check to see if my company was doing anything differently. Are we having any issue supplying my products, or did we change our strategy to focus on different brands?

"After I assessed those factors, I'd look at my marketing mix. First, I'd see if I changed my product formulations recently. Or did anything happen that reduced the quality of my products? Next, I'd look at pricing. Did I change my pricing strategy in a way that could be affecting my sales? Then, I'd look at my marketing promotions. Did I change my advertising messages or any of my media tactics? Finally, I'd see if anything changed in the places where I sell my products. Did I lose any points of distribution, or did my display presence change at all?

"When I get the answers to those questions, I could figure out what's causing my sales to decline. Then, I could address the specific issues that are causing the decline."

Jim looked amazed. "Wow. That was a lot better than my answer."

Jamal smiled. "Yes, it was. Recruiters are looking for someone who can think through a problem from multiple angles. That's why the marketing frameworks are so useful. They give you a structure so your answers can be more thorough than if you just say the first thing that comes to mind.

"Let's try a different case question. What's your favorite advertisement, and why?"

Jim thought for a moment. "I like the Smitty's Auto Brands ad that shows NASCAR drivers racing around auto parts stores. Since I'm a NASCAR fan, that ad really appeals to me."

Jamal said, "That's nice, but it doesn't make me want to hire you."

Jim was confused. "What do you mean? I answered your question."

"Yeah, but your answer wasn't very good. Here's how I'd answer the question using the 3C's framework." Jamal paused, then said, "Before I tell you which advertisement's my favorite, let me tell you the criteria I'd use. First, the ad should communicate a benefit that customers care about. Second, it should to break through the clutter of all the competitive ads. And third, it should have a positive impact on the company's sales.

"Using those criteria, my favorite ad is the Smitty's Auto Brands one that shows NASCAR drivers racing around the Smitty's auto parts store. It communicates how quickly customers can get their car parts because of the rapid drive-through lanes in every Smitty's location, and that's a benefit customers probably want. Next, it breaks through the clutter of competitive ads because of the cool special effects it uses to show drivers speeding through the drive-through lanes. And finally, it increased the company's sales. I read that since they started showing that ad, sales in Smitty's stores are up 5%. Because that ad delivered on all three of my criteria, it's my favorite."

Jim was silent. Finally, he said, "That was great, but I'm never gonna remember all that."

Jamal smiled. "You don't have to. Can you remember the 3C's?"

"Yes, of course. But the other stuff you said about offering relevant benefits and breaking through clutter … how can I keep track of all that?"

"It's easy. Just remember the 3C's. What do customers want? How can you be better than your competitors? And how is your company impacted? It takes some practice, but since those C's are the foundation of marketing, you can use them to answer almost any case question."

Jim smiled. "OK, I think I got it. But what about non-marketing questions? I'm in an interview group with people from healthcare, engineering, and computer science. Can they use the 3C's?"

"No, they really can't. Those career fields all have different frameworks, so they'll have to figure out how to answer their case questions using frameworks from their

7. CASE QUESTIONS

fields of study. We have career counselors who can help, or I'm sure their professors can give them advice." Jamal looked at his watch. "That's all the time we have for today. Just practice your case questions using the 3C's and 4P's. You can tell your friends to find the frameworks that'll work for the types of case questions they'll get."

Jamal walked Jim to the door and said goodbye. Jim went to the student lounge where he practiced his case questions while he waited for his other group members to arrive.

When they got there, Jim explained what he learned from Jamal. He expected Sarah, Abby, and Ethan to be overwhelmed, but they seemed to understand quickly.

Sarah started. "I think I get it. In medicine, we have all kinds of tricks to remember how to treat patients. One of them is called MONA. When we think someone might be having a heart attack, we're supposed to remember M for morphine, O for oxygen, N for nitroglycerin, and A for aspirin."

Abby jumped in. "Yeah, in engineering, we have something called SOLVE. When we have an engineering problem, we study the problem, organize the facts, line up the plan, verify the plan with computations, and examine the answer to make sure it's right. I bet I can use that mnemonic to answer engineering questions."

Ethan still looked a bit confused. "Abby, I didn't understand anything you just said, and I have no idea what a mnemonic is. But I think I understand how to answer a case question. They're like word problems in math class. You just have to translate the question into the steps needed to come up with a good answer. When I need to debug a program, I use an abbreviation called R.S.C.F.T. I like to call it re-scuft … like you scuff your shoes again. It stands for recognize that a bug exists, find the source of the bug, identify the cause, determine the fix, and test the fix."

Abby shook her head. "That's a mnemonic."

Ethan shrugged. "Whatever fancy name you give it, it works for me."

The group continued to talk about case questions for about an hour. Then they decided to find people in each of their majors to practice with. They spent the next few days working on their subject-specific case questions with the help of classmates, professors, and career counselors who were knowledgeable in each of their career fields.

At their next meeting, Jim said, "Let's each practice one case question from our list." He handed his list of marketing questions to Sarah and said, "Ask me any of these you want."

Sarah skimmed the list. "Here's a good one. If you're working on a brand, and your sales start to decline, what questions would you ask?"

Jim was pleased. That was a question he'd practiced several times over the past week. "I'd start with the 3C's, then move on to the 4P's.

"First, I'd begin with my customers. Have there been any changes in their purchasing behavior or their preferences that are impacting my sales? Then, I'd look at competitors. Have any of them launched any new products or changed their promotional strategies recently? Next, I'd look at my company. Have we changed the way we've prioritized our brands or have we reallocated resources across our initiatives?

"Then, I'd look at the 4P's. Have my products changed in any way? For example, did I reformulate anything or is the product quality going down for any reason? Next, I'd ask if I changed my pricing strategy. Am I charging more or are retailers putting my brand on sale less often? Then, I'd look at my promotions. Have I changed my marketing message or tactics recently?

Finally, I'd look at the placement of my products. Have I lost distribution, or am I losing shelf space in stores?

"Once I asked those questions, I'd assess what's happening to cause my brand's sales to decline. Then, I'd formulate a strategy to get my brand back on track."

"Nice," said Sarah. "I don't know much about marketing, but that sounded impressive to me." She turned to Abby. "Can you ask me one of the questions from my healthcare list?"

"OK." Abby looked over the list, then asked, "What would you do if a patient faints in front of you?"

Sarah answered, "For fainting, I'd use a mnemonic that I learned called L.A.R.C.

"First, I'd lay the person flat on their back. That's the L. Then, I'd check their airway, which is the A. If they weren't breathing, I'd administer CPR. Next, I'd try to revive them, which is the R. I could do that by tapping on their arm and talking to them loudly. If that didn't work, I'd call for help. That's the C.

"If at any time, they started to vomit, I'd turn them on their side to keep their airway clear. If they regained consciousness, I'd check to see if they might be dehydrated or if they might not have eaten in a while. If that were the

7. CASE QUESTIONS

case, I might try to get them to drink some water or some juice.

"Finally, I'd stay with them until they were fully recovered or until help arrived."

Ethan said, "Remind me that if I'm ever going to faint, I need to do it when you're around. It sounds like you really know what you're doing."

Sarah smiled. "Thanks. Now it's your turn. Hand me your list."

Ethan gave his computer science list to Sarah and braced himself for her question.

She looked at the list and asked, "If your boss told you to debug a program, how would you approach it?"

Ethan looked relieved. "Good, that's one I know the answer to. I'd use a process I call re-scuffed. It stands for recognize that a bug exists, find the source of the bug, identify the cause, determine the fix, and test the fix.

"Recognizing that a bug exists would be easy since my boss told me to fix it. To find the source, I'd test the program to see where it stops working when the bug occurs. Then, I'd find the cause of the bug by going into the source code to see where the program might be faulty. Then, I'd determine the fix by writing updated source code that is bug-free. Finally, I'd test the fix by re-running the program after I inserted the new code. If everything works, then I would have successfully debugged the program. If not, I'd go back to the beginning and do the re-scuffed process again until I fixed the error."

Sarah nodded her head. "Again, I didn't understand much of that, but it sounded good. Abby, you're the engineer. How did Ethan's answer sound to you?"

Abby replied, "Really good. I think he's ready for that question in a real interview. Now it's my turn. Jim, here's my list of questions. Ask me anything?"

Jim looked over the list and asked, "If I asked you to design a new highway intersection, how would you approach that?"

Abby said, "That's not one I've practiced yet, but I'll give it a try. If I had to design an intersection, I'd use a process called SOLVE. It stands for study the problem, organize the facts, line up the plan, verify the plan, and examine the answer.

"Here's how it works. First, I'd study the intersection to find any issues or opportunities for improving it. Then I'd organize facts like how much space I had to work with, how the traffic currently flowed through the intersection, and what the future needs might be. Next, I'd line up a plan, which could involve designing the number of lanes and whether stoplights might be needed. Then I'd verify the plan by calculating whether my new design would improve the traffic flow. Finally, I'd examine my answer to make sure my assumptions and calculations were correct. Once I did all that, I'd show my plan to a few traffic experts to see if they could find ways to improve it."

Ethan made a fist and held it up toward Abby. "Girl, that was awesome."

Abby gave Ethan a fist bump. "Thanks. I'm lovin' that SOLVE mnemonic. It seems to work for a lot of the engineering case questions."

The team agreed that they were ready to take on their interviews. They called it quits for the day and went to their classes.

***

As you can see from this story, case questions are much easier to answer when you have a framework in mind.

With case questions, recruiters want to see if you can think through challenging problems or address situations that might come up in the jobs they're trying to fill. Since those situations are specific to particular types of jobs, you should practice your case answers with people who are knowledgeable in your career field.

Often, student organizations are the best resources for practicing case answers. For example, when I was in business school, our marketing club hosted workshops for case questions. During those sessions, we met with other marketing students to improve our answers together. We'd also get coaching from upperclassmen, professors, and recruiters who specialized in marketing.

If your school's student organization for your major doesn't host case interview workshops, you might want to organize one. It's a good way to build your skills. Plus, it will give you a great S-T-A-R story to highlight your leadership abilities.

Here are a few dos and don'ts for case questions:

Dos:
- Use a framework that's relevant for your field of study. In our story, Jim used the 3C's marketing framework. The other characters used frameworks for healthcare, engineering, and computer science. Find out what frameworks are common in your major, and practice answering case questions using those frameworks.

- Consider telling the interviewer what your criteria will be for your answer. That will demonstrate you can make decisions based on clear, compelling criteria.
- If you don't have an immediate answer to the question, ask a few clarifying questions. That will demonstrate you can seek to understand a situation rather than jumping straight to an answer without understanding the context. Asking a few clarifying questions will also buy you time to think of your answer.

Don'ts:
- Don't give a short, one-sentence answer. If rush through your response, you could be seen as impulsive or lacking a depth of knowledge. You want to show recruiters that you can logically formulate a thoughtful recommendation.
- Don't act like your answer is the only correct one. You might come off as arrogant or rigid if you act like your answer is the only option.

I recommend you take a few minutes now to think about how you'd answer case questions for your line of work. Think about some of the frameworks and mnemonics that are common in your career field. If you need help, just look in your introductory text books or do an internet search. You can also get ideas from career counselors, professors, and members of your interview group.

See page 187 for templates and examples to help you practice for case questions.

7. CASE QUESTIONS

8. Nail the Interviews

Your next objective should be to get recruiters to add you to their interview schedules. For recruiters who come on campus, your school's career development office might manage their interview process. Make sure you know the steps required to request interviews with those recruiters. Steps could include submitting your resume to your career development office and possibly bidding for interview slots.

If your school doesn't have a formalized process, you may need to contact recruiters directly. If that's the case, see if you can find each recruiter's preferred form of communication. Some recruiters want you to email them a copy of your resume along with a short explanation of the job you're applying for. Others may want you to fill out an online employment application and upload your resume to their jobs website. If you're unsure of the proper process, feel free to contact the company via email or phone call. Most companies will include their contact information on their websites.

Once you get on the interview schedules, the trick will be to show up to your interviews relaxed and prepared. If you've followed the steps in this book, you should be in good shape. Remember, the more practice you've done, the more prepared you'll be. Like any competition, the winning prize goes to the competitors who've practiced the most, who've developed the best skills, and who perform the best on the day of the competition.

There should be no need for you to stay up late the night before cramming for the interview. Since you've been practicing for weeks, possibly months, it'll be more important for you to show up for the interview well-rested. Do anything you can to relax and get a good night's sleep before the interview.

On the interview day, make sure you dress appropriately and show up ten to fifteen minutes before your interview. If the recruiter is running ahead of schedule, they'll be impressed that you're ready early. If they're running late, you'll have extra time to relax in the waiting room before your interview starts.

When it's your time to interview, greet the recruiter with a friendly smile and a firm handshake. As a recruiter, I always enjoy seeing friendly, cheerful people.

Let the recruiter set the pace for the interview. They may want to start with small talk, they may want to tell you about themselves, or they may want to just jump right into the interview questions.

Remember to be calm and positive from the start of the interview to the end. Recruiters are looking for people who can be engaging and professional in any situation, so be friendly but not too informal.

If they ask you to tell them about yourself or walk them through your resume, you're in luck. You'll nail those questions since you've practiced them so many times.

If they start with different questions, don't worry. You can adjust to any question they ask because you've done a great job preparing.

After you answer all the interview questions brilliantly, the recruiter may ask, "Do you have any questions for me?" This is your opportunity to get them into selling mode. You want them to start telling you why their organization is a great place to work. My favorite response to this question is, "What do you like most about working for your company?" When I'm interviewing candidates and I hear that question, I automatically start thinking about why that candidate would want to work for my company. Then, I start picturing them in my organization, and I think about what I should say to get them to accept a job offer.

8. NAIL THE INTERVIEWS

Let's see how the characters in our story handle this final stage in the process.

* * *

Jim was nervous when he arrived for his weekly meeting with Billy. With only a few weeks until his first interview, he didn't feel prepared.

Billy greeted him with a handshake. "Jimbo, we're in the final stretch. How did it go with Jamal last week?"

"It went well. He was great. I'm just worried that I'm not ready yet."

"I'll be the judge of that. Today, we'll be doing a practice interview. That'll be your final exam for our counseling sessions. When our practice interview is done, we'll make sure you're on track to get onto the right interview schedules."

Billy guided Jim to a conference room where they sat down. Then Billy started asking interview questions, and Jim responded to every question with clear, well-structured answers. After Jim answered the last question, Billy smiled and said, "That's it. You're ready."

Jim asked, "How did I do? Did I pass?"

"I'd say you earned an A+," Billy replied. "You're ready for anything they can throw at you." Billy then coached Jim through the process to get onto interview schedules. "Your top three companies are coming to campus for interviews in a few weeks. You'll need to submit your resume to them using our online process. Your number four and five companies aren't coming here, so just send your resume directly to them. Go ahead and send your resume to your safety companies too. I don't think you'll need them based on how you interviewed today, but better safe than sorry." Billy gave Jim a few more tips, then sent him on his way.

Jim went to the student lounge where he found Ethan and Abby practicing their interview questions. He walked over to them and said, "You're here early. We don't meet for another hour."

Ethan responded, "We know. Abby has an interview tomorrow, so we're getting in a little extra practice."

Abby gestured to an empty chair at their table. "Grab a seat. I could use another sounding board. Ethan's in bad-cop mode today. I'm hoping you can be good-cop."

Jim smiled and sat down. He and Ethan asked Abby questions and evaluated her answers until Sarah arrived. Then they split up into pairs with Ethan and Abby staying

8. NAIL THE INTERVIEWS

at their table, and Jim and Sarah going to another. After two more hours of practice, they all left to get on with their days.

The group continued to meet for the next few weeks, putting the finishing touches on their interview answers. They also helped each other with wording for cover letters and online applications, and they gave each other pep talks as interviews approached.

Abby was the first to hear back from recruiters. She received offers from her top two companies. Her #3 company sent her an email saying she advanced to their second round interviews, which later led to another offer. In the end, she received four offers. She accepted the offer from the company she originally ranked #3 on her list because they impressed her the most during the interview process.

Ethan wasn't as successful. His #1 and #2 companies didn't come to campus, and they didn't respond to his inquiries. He interviewed with his next two choices and only got a second round interview with his #4 choice. He nailed that call-back interview, got an offer, and quickly accepted it.

Sarah was next. She got a rejection letter from her #3 company, then she received offers from her top two choices. She quickly accepted the offer from her #1 company.

Jim was last in the process. He bombed the interview for is #2 choice, Kickalot Sporting Goods. After the interview, he met with Ethan. "I don't understand," Jim said. "I completely froze. It didn't help that they asked all kinds of questions about sports gear. I don't think they wanted a marketer. I think they just wanted someone who likes sports."

Ethan seemed sympathetic. "It's their loss. If they don't give you an offer, they don't know what they're missing. Let's go over your questions again. You've got Smitty's Auto Brands tomorrow, so I want to hear your best material."

They spent the next two hours practicing as Ethan asked Jim questions, listened to his responses, and offered feedback. Finally, Ethan said, "It's seven o'clock, and you need to get some rest. What time is your interview with Smitty's tomorrow?"

"Nine a.m.," Jim responded.

Ethan and Jim stood up and walked out of the lounge together.

The next day, Jim woke up early, ate a big breakfast, and walked around campus to clear his head before the

8. NAIL THE INTERVIEWS

interview. He thought about the past few months, and he realized how much he'd learned. When he got to campus at the beginning of the school year, he was lost. He had no idea how to get a good job. After the coaching sessions with Billy and dozens of hours of practice with his interview group, he should be ready. Why did he still feel nervous?

He arrived at the career development office fifteen minutes before his interview. The waiting room was buzzing with other students waiting for their interviews. Jim saw Emily from his debate team and started to talk with her. "Emily, I thought you had an offer from Hydropoly-something? What are you doing here?"

"I'm interviewing with another biotech company. They're in Miami, and I couldn't resist talking with them. How about you? Who are you interviewing with?"

"Smitty's Auto Brands. They're only my top choice."

"Nice. I love their ad with the NASCAR drivers. Well, good luck," Emily said as a recruiter called her name.

When it was his turn, Jim went to the interview room with the recruiter from Smitty's. Forty-five minutes later, he walked out. What a rush. He nailed every question. His response to "tell me about yourself" was amazing, he told his best S-T-A-R stories, and his answers to the case questions were brilliant.

Two days later, Jim received an email from the Smitty's recruiter. It was an offer to be their next marketing intern. He immediately replied back with his acceptance.

In the end, all four members of Jim's interview group received offers for great summer jobs, and those jobs got them on track for amazing careers in their respective fields. And to think, it all started with Jim asking someone, "What should I be doing differently?" That simple question led to him to becoming amazing at answering interview questions, which resulted in him getting his top choice for a summer job.

With his newfound confidence, Jim wondered what he should do next. He picked up his phone and called Sarah. When she answered, Jim asked, "Sarah, would you like to have dinner with me tomorrow night?"

On the other end of the call, Sarah smiled.

* * *

That's it. That's the plan you'll need to get your career started. If you form your interview group, practice your skills, and nail your interviews, you'll be all set. It may seem like a lot, but just take it one step at a time and you'll be fine.

8. NAIL THE INTERVIEWS

Remember, Jim didn't know how to start. That's where I was when I got to business school. I had no idea what I needed to do to get great job. Fortunately, someone told me to form an interview group. That was the best career advice I've ever gotten. I did what they said, and before I graduated, I got job offers from all five of the top companies on my list. While I can't promise you'll go five for five on your top choices, I can promise you'll be better off if you follow the advice in this book.

I also spent a lot of time in my school's career development office. Hopefully, you'll find a great career counselor at your school. If not, you can still follow the other steps in this book.

You have so many options for finding the information you need to get a dream job. Just track down what you need from student organizations, professors, recruiters, and anyone else you can find. There are also hundreds of good websites with useful job information.

Most importantly, you should find a way to make job hunting and interview practice part of your routine. It's like anything else. If you have a good plan, you'll be off to a great start. If you dedicate time and effort to it, you'll become even better. This book gives you a good plan. The question is whether you'll dedicate the time and effort needed to become great.

See page 199 for a checklist of tips to help you nail your interviews.

8. NAIL THE INTERVIEWS

Conclusion

Here's a summary of the game plan I've described in this book.

Step 1: Form an Interview Group. Your best resources for getting a great job will be your peers. By forming an interview group, you'll create a team of people who will help you build your job hunting strategy, polish your resume, and practice your interview skills. Most importantly, by committing to an interview group, you'll have people who will hold you accountable for your progress.

Make sure you choose people who are motivated. If you find that someone in your group doesn't show up or doesn't want to do the work, it's OK to kick them out. Not everyone wants to put forth the effort needed to get the best jobs. You should surround yourself with people who are willing to work hard. That will create a culture of success, which will be important if you're going after the best jobs in your field.

Also, remember to find people who you enjoy being around. Interview groups should be fun, so make sure your group is filled with people you want to spend time with.

Step 2: Build Your Job Hunting Strategy. During this phase, you'll research your career field to make sure it's right for you. If not, this is a good time to change your major so you don't spend years going down the wrong path.

Once you're sure you've chosen the right career for you, start researching organizations that hire people in your field of interest. You can do this with the help of your school's career development office, student organizations, and professors. You can also talk with other students who are majoring in the same subject as you.

As you evaluate potential employers, start categorizing them into tiers. Your top tier will include employers that are the best fit for your professional and personal goals. Other potential employers can be included in your second tier or your list of safety companies. If you can't get into your top tier choices, these other companies might still be good places to start your career.

As you identify potential employers, take notes on the names and contact information for their recruiters as well as their interview dates. Those notes will ensure you know who to contact and when to interview with each organization.

Also, make sure you find job descriptions from your top tier employers. Those job descriptions will be your cheat sheets as you polish your resume and practice your interview skills.

Step 3: Polish Your Resume. The secret to a good resume is using a job description to write it. Your resume should include any experience you have that relates to the job description for the job you want.

For each experience you put on your resume, list the actions you've done and the results you've gotten that are most like those on the job description. Recruiters are looking for people whose experiences line up with the role they're hiring for. As such, make sure your resume lines up as closely as possible with the recruiters' job descriptions.

Also, remember to include a few eye-catching interests at the bottom of your resume. Those interests may entice a recruiter to add you to their interview list because they have something in common with you or they're curious about something you've done.

Step 4: Get a List of Interview Questions. This is the easiest step in the process. Since most recruiters ask the same types of questions, you can start with the list of interview questions on my website. Just go to AmazingJobSkills.com and download the questions. You can find them by clicking on the "Templates" link that's in the menu at the top of the home page. You can also contact your school's career development office, student organizations, and even potential employers to see if they have lists of interview questions.

There are hundreds of books that include lists of interview questions. My favorite is *Amazing Interview Answers* by yours truly. Yes, I am biased. However, I won't be offended if you use other sources to get your list of interview questions, as long as you have a good list to work with.

Step 5: Practice the Opening Questions. The most important interview question is typically the one recruiters start with, which is "tell me about yourself." You should absolutely nail this question. Since you know it's coming, you should have an amazing answer for it.

I recommend you use the P-E-N framework to tell the recruiter what you're passionate about, what relevant experiences you have, and what you want to do next. Make sure your passion, experiences, and next line up with the job you want.

Remember, recruiters are trying to find people who will love working for their organizations. Therefore, when you're practicing for this question, look at the recruiter's job description and tell them why you'll be passionate about doing the tasks on that job description.

You can also use the P-E-N framework to answer other opening questions including "walk me through your resume, why are you interested in this job, and why should I hire you."

Step 6: Practice the Fit Questions. When recruiters ask you fit questions, you should be ready with a variety of good answers that use the S-T-A-R framework. That means you should have stories that highlight the situations, tasks, actions, and results from your past experiences.

I recommend you start with your four or five biggest accomplishments. For each of them, write down one sentence that describes the situation, which could include your job title and the organization you were in. Then, write down your task, which could be the assignment or goal you had. Then, list the two or three actions you took to accomplish that task. Finally, write down the result you got, and try to state that result is a way that's as measurable as possible.

This S-T-A-R technique will make your answer interesting for recruiters since it will give them a story about you that has a beginning, a middle, and an end. It will also show them that you can work towards a goal, take necessary actions, and get meaningful results.

You should choose S-T-A-R stories from your past that highlight the type of work you want to do. If you're in a creative field, practice telling stories about the times you've delivered creative results. If you're in an analytical field, your stories should highlight your analytical skills.

Step 7: Practice the Case Questions. This is the trickiest part of the process. Since case questions are different for every type of career field, you'll have to do a little extra research to develop good answers to these questions.

Currently, there are a variety of books available about case questions for technology, consulting, and healthcare jobs. If you're in another field, you might need to look harder to find good questions. I've included a few case questions in my *Amazing Interview Answers* book, but you'll likely need more if you're in a case-oriented field. If so, see if your school's career development office, student organizations, or professors have case questions you can use. Once you get a good list of questions, practice your answers with other people in your career field.

Step 8: Nail the Interviews. The final step of the process is to nail your interviews. Most employers use the interviews as the primary factor when considering candidates for jobs. Sure, a good resume or a compelling cover letter might get you into an interview, but it's the interview itself that will determine whether you get a job offer.

As such, make sure you're well-rested and well-prepared for your interviews. Show up on your interview day dressed appropriately and ready to dazzle the recruiter.

The best way to perform well in interviews is to have plenty of practice ahead of time. In addition to the practice sessions with your interview group, I recommend you schedule several mock interviews with counselors in your school's career development office. Or, see if there are upperclassmen or college professors who will interview

CONCLUSION

you before your interviews with recruiters. That way, you'll get used to being in a situation with people who have experience assessing interview answers.

Remember, if your priority is to get a good job, you should commit the time and effort needed to prepare. This book gives you the game plan. You just need to execute that plan.

That's it. That's all you need to get started. Now, go out and form your interview group. They'll help you get the practice you'll need to become a great interview candidate.

Best wishes as you start your career.

I do have one final request. Please take a minute to rate this book on the site where you bought it and write a review to tell other students what you think of it. Your review will really help me get awareness for this book.

Reference Materials

REFERENCE MATERIALS

Step 1: Form an Interview Group

Use this page to plan your interview group meetings. Write down the names of people who may be motivated to join your group and who you enjoy spending time with. They can be people from your classes, student organizations, fraternity, sorority, or anywhere else you can find potential members. Circle the names of the people you invite if they accept your invitation.

Name	Email Address	Phone Number
_____	_____	_____
_____	_____	_____
_____	_____	_____
_____	_____	_____
_____	_____	_____
_____	_____	_____

Meeting Dates and Times: _____
_____

Dates and Times to Practice Alone: _____
_____

REFERENCE MATERIALS

Step 2: Build Your Job Hunting Strategy

Use this page to plan your interview strategy. Write down your criteria for the places you want to work and the names of the organizations that fit those criteria.

Criteria (career, cultural, and geographic priorities): _____
_____
_____

<u>Organization</u>　　<u>Recruiter Name & Contact Info</u>　　<u>Interview Date(s)</u>

Top Tier:

1. _____　　_____　　_____

2. _____　　_____　　_____

3. _____　　_____　　_____

Other Options:

1. _____　　_____　　_____

2. _____　　_____　　_____

3. _____　　_____　　_____

REFERENCE MATERIALS

Step 3: Polish Your Resume

This section includes a template for you to build your resume as well as five sample resumes for the characters in this book. Start by listing the key responsibilities and tasks from the job descriptions of your top tier organizations.

Job Description Tasks

_____

_____

_____

_____

_____

_____

_____

_____

_____

_____

REFERENCE MATERIALS

Sample Job Descriptions

Education: Job Description for Billy's Targeted Internship
- Tutor individual students who need extra help
- Assist teachers with lesson planning
- Maintain order in classrooms
- Grade assignments and exams
- Prepare written evaluations summarizing abilities for students

Business: Job Description for Jim's Targeted Internship
- Analyze data to identify opportunities for new products
- Conduct research and build business plans to increase sales
- Lead cross-functional teams to develop new marketing campaigns
- Lead agency partners to develop marketing and sales materials
- Manage timelines and budgets

Nursing: Job Description for Sarah's Targeted Internship
- Measure patients' vital signs
- Record patients' medical histories and health concerns
- Assist patients with moving about the facility
- Feed, bathe, and dress patients
- Observe and record changes in patients' conditions

Engineering: Job Description for Abby's Targeted Internship
- Develop engineering plans and designs for structures and systems
- Conduct inspections and tests to ensure the quality of construction
- Prepare budgets and identify cost saving opportunities
- Write reports to recommend engineering solutions
- Conduct research and provide technical assistance to engineers

Computers: Job Description for Ethan's Targeted Internship
- Code, test, and debug programming for software applications
- Analyze and recommend improvements to computer networks
- Identify and repair technical issues
- Install and trouble-shoot computer hardware and software
- Address technical support requests from employees
- Lead training for computer hardware and software

REFERENCE MATERIALS

Resume Template

Your Name: _____

Street Address: _____

Email address: _____, phone number: _____

EDUCATION

UNIVERSITY NAME, City, State: _____

Degree: _____

Anticipated Graduation: _____

School Activities, Offices Held, Honors, or Major Awards: _____

_____

_____

EXPERIENCE

EMPLOYER NAME (most recent): _____

Time Period Worked (example: 2017-2018): _____

Job Title (most recent): _____

- Action and result: _____

   _____

- Action and result: _____

   _____

- Action and result: _____

   _____

EMPLOYER NAME (most recent): _____

Time Period Worked (example: 2017-2018): _____

Job Title (most recent): _____

- Action and result: _____
  _____

- Action and result: _____
  _____

- Action and result: _____
  _____

EMPLOYER NAME (most recent): _____

Time Period Worked (example: 2017-2018): _____

Job Title (most recent): _____

- Action and result: _____
  _____

- Action and result: _____
  _____

- Action and result: _____
  _____

ADDITIONAL INFORMATION

Major awards, volunteer positions, and/or interests

- _____
- _____
- _____

REFERENCE MATERIALS

William "Billy" Jackson

985 8th Street, Apt 23, University City, SC 29910
w.jackson@southernstate.edu, 843-555-8743

EDUCATION

SOUTHERN STATE UNIVERSITY, University City, SC
Bachelor of Science in Education, Emphasis in Secondary Education
Anticipated Graduation May 2019
Career Counselor at Office of Career Development

EXPERIENCE

HILLSIDE EXPLORERS CAMP
Senior Camp Counselor   Summer 2017

- Tutored 25 camp attendees to improve their skills with writing, crafts, and outdoor survival
- Assisted camp director with lesson planning for 5 summer camp activities
- Maintained order among 60+ teenage students during classroom sessions and outdoor training exercises
- Coached students in basketball, soccer, and various physical fitness activities

Camp Counselor   Summer 2016

- Graded crafts projects and writing assignments for over 50 camp attendees
- Helped maintain order among 30+ teenage students during classroom sessions and outdoor training exercises
- Prepared written evaluations to communicate progress to students and parents

ADDITIONAL INFORMATION

- Volunteer and basketball coach at Boys & Girls Club
- Winner of Middleton High School talent contest
- Interests: Basketball, chess, and collecting rare books

Jim Harrison

1212 College Avenue, Apt 3B, University City, SC 29910
j.harrison@southernstate.edu, 843-555-1212

EDUCATION

SOUTHERN STATE UNIVERSITY, University City, SC
Bachelor of Arts in Business, Emphasis in Marketing
Anticipated Graduation May 2020
Communication Committee Chair for Debate Team

EXPERIENCE

HILLSIDE EXPLORERS CAMP
Camp Communications Manager   Summer 2018
- Analyzed data from competitive camps to identify four new activity offerings
- Conducted research among camp attendees and parents to identify new marketing strategy and campaign elements projected to increase applications by 40%
- Led cross-functional team of counselors, activity directors, and foodservice managers to develop new online strategy that delivered over 50% increase in site traffic

Camp Counselor   Summer 2017
- Led agency partners in development of camp's first-ever social media site and direct mail campaign that generated 30% increase in applications
- Managed timelines and budgets for development of three new camp activities

ADDITIONAL INFORMATION

- Webmaster for University City Running Club website (ucrc.run)
- Interests: Running, reading books about psychology, and producing videos (produced YouTube videos with over 5 million combined views)

Sarah Barker

219 Center Street, University City, SC 29910
s.barker@southernstate.edu, 843-444-2323

EDUCATION

SOUTHERN STATE UNIVERSITY, University City, SC
Bachelor of Science Dual Degree in Nursing & Psychology
Anticipated Graduation May 2020
Vice President for the Student Healthcare Club

EXPERIENCE

UNIVERSITY CITY MEDICAL CENTER
Volunteer Nursing Assistant   Summer 2018

- Measured vital signs and medical histories for over 200 patients
- Trained 15 nurses and medical assistants on new software for recording medical records; saved company $10,000 in training costs
- Designed and implemented new check-in process that reduced waiting times by 30%

PLEASANTON RETIREMENT HOME
Summer Orderly   Summer 2017

- Assisted patients with moving around facility, including pushing wheelchairs and taking patients for walks
- Fed, bathed, and dressed patients
- Observed and recorded changes in patients' physical, mental, and emotional conditions
- Recognized as Employee of the Month for receiving top scores on surveys completed by patients and family members

ADDITIONAL INFORMATION

- Volunteer and social media coordinator for Hearts for Children charitable organization
- Interests: travel, cooking, and tennis
- Fluent in English, Spanish, and French

Abby Walker

915 Highland Circle, Apt 22, University City, SC 29910
a.walker@southernstate.edu, 843-333-9876

EDUCATION

SOUTHERN STATE UNIVERSITY, University City, SC
Bachelor of Science in Engineering
Anticipated Graduation May 2020
Treasurer for Physics Club
Staff reporter for school newspaper

EXPERIENCE

UNIVERSITY CITY ANIMAL SHELTER
Assistant Office Manager   Summer 2018
- Developed engineering plans for new kennel system that gives each animal 30% more living space within existing building structure
- Conducted inspections and tests to ensure new kennel system will be structurally sound
- Prepared budgets and identified cost savings measures that reduce cost of new kennel system by over $20,000

HOMES FOR HUMANS VOLUNTEER
Summer Construction Volunteer   Summer 2017
- Wrote reports to recommend improvements for construction techniques that are projected to reduce maintenance cost by 20%
- Conducted research on building materials and identified higher-quality options that would reduce material costs by 20%
- Performed construction inspections to ensure building structures met specifications

ADDITIONAL INFORMATION

- Winner of Centerville High School Science Fair
- Interests: robotics and martial arts (black belt in taekwondo)

Ethan Wright

708 Beacon Street, University City, SC 29910

e.wright@southernstate.edu, 843-444-2468

EDUCATION

SOUTHERN STATE UNIVERSITY, University City, SC
Bachelor of Science in Computer Science
Anticipated Graduation May 2020
Winner of Computer Club's Annual Programming Competition

EXPERIENCE

THE WRIGHT ELECTRONICS STORE

Computer Programming Technician   2017 - present

- Coded, tested, and debugged software applications used by over 500 employees to record sales and track inventory
- Analyzed and installed improvements to computer networks that reduced downtimes by an average of 80%
- Identified and repaired technical issues with existing software applications to improve system efficiency by over 20%

Computer Repair Technician   2015 - 2017

- Installed and ensured proper functioning of computer hardware and software for over 100 customers
- Addressed over 50 technical support requests from employees and customers
- Led 4 training sessions on new computer software applications for employees and customers

ADDITIONAL INFORMATION

- Volunteer troop leader for Boy Scouts of America
- Eagle Scout: final project involved designing and installing a new computer network for Franklin High School in Greentown, SC
- Interests: blog writing, photography, and playing the guitar

Step 4: List of Interview Questions

This section includes a list of common interview questions.

Opening Questions

1. Tell me about yourself.
2. Walk me through your resume.
3. What makes you a good choice for this job?
4. Why are you interested in this job?
5. Why should I hire you?
6. Where do you see yourself in five years?
7. Describe your dream job.
8. Why do you want to leave your current job?
9. What do you know about our organization?
10. What do you know about the job you're applying for?

Fit Questions

1. What is your biggest strength?
2. What is your biggest weakness?
3. Tell me about a time when you've demonstrated creativity.
4. Tell me about a time when you've demonstrated analytical skills.
5. Tell me about a time when you've demonstrated persistence.
6. Tell me about a time when you've demonstrated leadership.
7. Tell me about a time when you've demonstrated collaboration.
8. Tell me about your leadership style.
9. How would a friend describe you?
10. Tell me about your biggest achievement.

REFERENCE MATERIALS

Case Questions

Case questions are specific to particular career fields. As such, here are examples of case questions for a few common types of jobs:

Education Case Questions:
1. How would you handle a parent who wants constant updates on their child's progress?
2. If you had a disruptive student in your class, what would you do?
3. How would you teach a child to add fractions if they didn't understand how to do it?
4. If you had to design a new lesson plan for your favorite subject, how would you do it?

Business Case Questions:
1. If your brand's sales start to decline, what questions would you ask?
2. You discover that some of your products are defective. What do you do?
3. You have to make a decision between investing in advertising, reducing your prices, or improving your product quality. How do you make that decision?
4. How would you determine the size of the market for a specific type of product?

Healthcare Case Questions:
1. You have a patient who faints. What do you do?
2. List the risk factors related to diabetes.
3. What is your favorite medication, and why?
4. How would you address a patient who is experiencing a sudden drop in blood pressure?

Write your answer to this question here.

PASSION: _____

_____

_____

EXPERIENCE: _____

_____

_____

_____

_____

_____

_____

_____

_____

_____

NEXT: _____

_____

_____

_____

_____

REFERENCE MATERIALS

Opening Question #2:
Walk Me Through Your Resume

Here's Sarah's answer to this question in a healthcare interview:

"As I walk you through my resume, I'll highlight a theme, which is my passion for helping people.

"Going chronologically from the bottom of my resume upwards, you'll see that my interests include foreign languages and travel. I've always enjoyed those things because they help me understand people from different backgrounds.

"My first volunteer experience was with an organization called Hearts for Children. That's where I became interested in healthcare. I really admired the way the nurses and psychologists helped kids who were dealing with illnesses. Since then, I've had two summer jobs that I've absolutely loved. The first was as an orderly at a retirement home where I did everything from feeding patients to helping them get around the facilities. The second was as a nursing assistant at a big medical center. In addition to performing my regular duties, I learned a new software program they were installing, and I trained fifteen nurses on the program. You'll also see that I'm getting a dual degree in nursing and psychology, which should help me pursue my passion for helping people.

"Now I'm looking for a position where I can help people while they're being treated at medical facilities. Based on my research, I think your organization will be a great place for me to do that."

Fit Question #2:
What Is Your Biggest Weakness?

Here's Sarah's answer to this question in a healthcare interview:

"I'd say my biggest weakness has been my hesitancy to be assertive. I have a diplomatic style, and I'm working on being more assertive when needed. Let me give you an example from when I was an orderly at the Pleasanton Retirement Home. One of my tasks was to transition patients from a common area to their rooms at the end of each day.

"One time, there was an elderly woman who wasn't willing to leave the common area. I tried every diplomatic approach I could think of to coax her to her room. Nothing worked. Finally, another orderly came in and firmly told the woman that she had to go to her room or she'd lose the privilege of coming to the common area the next day. I originally thought that threatening a resident like that might seem rude, but it worked in that situation.

"As a result, I've learned to be more assertive when needed. I still start with a diplomatic approach, but I'm more willing to become assertive if the situation calls for it."

Note: This is a difficult question to answer. I recommend you choose a weakness that's not a deal-breaker in your career field. Since nurses should be very diplomatic, Sarah's answer is a good one. She also does a great job of explaining how she's working to overcome that weakness.

Write your answer to this question here.

SITUATION: _____
_____

TASK: _____
_____

ACTIONS: _____
_____
_____
_____
_____
_____
_____
_____
_____
_____
_____

RESULT: _____
_____
_____

REFERENCE MATERIALS

Fit Question #1:
What Is Your Biggest Strength?

Here's Jim's answer to this question in a marketing interview:

"My biggest strength is my ability to identify opportunities that other people might miss. Let me give you an example from when I volunteered to be the webmaster for our university's running club. My task was to use our website to increase participation at our monthly fun runs.

"First, I did some research and learned that most students weren't even aware that we had a running club on campus., but they'd be interested in our fun runs if they knew about them ahead of time. Next, I created social media sites for our running club on Facebook, Instagram, and Twitter. Then, I posted weekly articles about the events on our social media feeds. Those articles drove traffic to our social media sites where students could sign up for our races.

"The result was a 300% increase in participation for our fun runs. I was able to get that result because I looked beyond our club's website and found opportunities to use social media to get some more people to our events."

Step 6: Practice the Fit Questions

In this section, you'll find five commonly asked fit questions along with a great answer for each question and a template for you to enter your own answer to each question.

REFERENCE MATERIALS

Write your answer to this question here.

PASSION: _____
_____
_____

EXPERIENCE: _____
_____
_____
_____
_____
_____
_____
_____
_____
_____

NEXT: _____
_____
_____
_____
_____

REFERENCE MATERIALS

Opening Question #5:
Why Should I Hire You?

Here's Billy's answer to this question in an education interview:

"You should hire me because of my passion for working with kids. I also have the experience needed to demonstrate I can be effective at teaching and motivating them.

"As you can see from my resume, I've spent two summers as a camp counselor. During that time, I've worked with over a hundred kids between the ages of ten and thirteen. My favorite part of that job was helping those kids improve their skills. My specialty was taking complicated tasks, like setting up an overnight campsite, and breaking it down into easy-to-understand steps. When I was hired to come back for my second summer, I was promoted to Senior Camp Counselor. I was given more responsibility and larger class sizes. In addition to teaching survival skills, I became the lead instructor for writing and crafts classes, and I coached several sports including basketball and soccer.

"As I said, I love working with kids, especially kids between the ages of ten and thirteen. Now I'm looking to start my career as a middle school teaching assistant or substitute teacher. You should hire me because I come with the passion and the experience you're looking for if you want someone who can connect with kids in this age range."

Write your answer to this question here.

PASSION: _____

_____

_____

EXPERIENCE: _____

_____

_____

_____

_____

_____

_____

_____

_____

_____

NEXT: _____

_____

_____

_____

REFERENCE MATERIALS

Opening Question #4:
Why Are You Interested in This Job?

Here's Ethan's answer to this question in a computer science interview:

"I've always been passionate about diagnosing and fixing computer problems. From what I read in the job description for this position, it looks like you want someone who can diagnose issues and develop improvements for software programs. If I understand correctly, you also want someone who can resolve technical issues with computer networks. That's exactly the kind of work I love doing.

"For the past few summers, I've worked at a computer store coding and debugging software applications. I've also analyzed computer networks and installed improvements to make them run more effectively. As you can see from my resume, I've been able to find ways to reduce network downtimes by an average of 80%. I've also worked with customers to address their technical service requests, and I really enjoy this type of work.

"Now I'm looking for a job where I can work with employees to help them with their technical issues. I'm also looking for opportunities to train people to use their computers more effectively. My understanding is that you're looking for people to do that type of work. I'd like to be part of your company since you're offering the kind of work I enjoy most."

Write your answer to this question here.

PASSION: _____

_____

_____

EXPERIENCE: _____

_____

_____

_____

_____

_____

_____

_____

_____

_____

NEXT: _____

_____

_____

_____

Opening Question #3:
Why Are You a Good Choice for This Job?

Here's Abby's answer to this question in an engineering interview:

"I'm a good choice because of my passion for solving complicated problems. From what I read in the job description for this position, it looks like you want someone who can solve a variety of complicated problems including developing engineering plans, conducting inspections, and preparing budgets. Here's what makes me good at these things.

"I take a very structured, logical approach to problem solving. For example, I won first place in the engineering category of my high school's annual science fair. In my project, I researched over a hundred building techniques and developed a system that delivers a 5% increase in weight bearing ability compared to today's most commonly used techniques for bridge building.

"As you can see on my resume, I also have experience in everything from developing improvements for construction techniques to creating engineering plans for dog kennels. I'm the treasurer for our university's physics club, which is helping me build my budgeting skills, and I'm a staff reporter for our school's newspaper, which helps me polish my writing skills.

"Now I'm looking for a position where I can apply my passion to solve even more complicated problems. That passion and my problem solving skills will make me a great choice for this job."

Write your answer to this question here.

PASSION: _____

_____

_____

EXPERIENCE: _____

_____

_____

_____

_____

_____

_____

_____

_____

_____

NEXT: _____

_____

_____

_____

_____

Write your answer to this question here.

SITUATION: _____

_____

TASK: _____

_____

ACTIONS: _____

_____

_____

_____

_____

_____

_____

_____

_____

_____

RESULT: _____

_____

_____

REFERENCE MATERIALS

Fit Question #3:
Tell Me About a Time When You Demonstrated Creativity

Here's Abby's answer to this question in an engineering interview:

"Last summer, I was an assistant office manager at an animal shelter. My task was to find a way to increase the number of dogs we could keep in our kennel building.

"I started by researching places where populations were becoming more dense. I noticed that in cities, people often lived in high-rise buildings, and they often lived with multiple people in small apartments. I decided to apply those lessons to our dog kennels. I designed kennels that could be stacked on top of each other so we could fit more kennels in the same space. I also researched which dog breeds and genders were most likely to coexist peacefully in the same living space. I built prototype kennel-apartments and tested them with a variety of dogs. After weeks of testing, I made adjustments to the designs, and I supervised a contractor who converted all our small-dog kennels to my new apartment-style design.

"Because I found a creative solution, the result was a 40% increase in the number of dogs that could be housed in our kennel building. As an added benefit, I discovered that the dogs that moved in with roommates were less aggressive and more playful. We noticed that those dogs were 10% more likely to get adopted because their behavior appealed to people who came to our facility looking to find a pet."

Write your answer to this question here.

SITUATION: _____
_____

TASK: _____
_____

ACTIONS: _____
_____
_____
_____
_____
_____
_____
_____
_____
_____
_____
_____

RESULT: _____
_____
_____

Fit Question #4:
Tell Me About a Time When You Used Your Analytical Skills

Here's Ethan's answer to this question in a computer science interview:

"When I was in high school, I was working to get my Eagle Scout certification. For my final project, I chose to design and install a new computer network for my high school. I chose that project because of my passion for computers and because our school's network was frequently going down.

"I started by calculating the data usage for the existing network. I learned that our bandwidth usage was 50% higher than other high school of similar size. I also learned that our usage had doubled every year for the past five years. Then, I projected the bandwidth needs for the next five years and determined how much the network would need to expand over time. I used that information to design a network that could handle the current usage needs and be expandable to handle future needs. Since we only needed the bandwidth from 8:00 a.m. to 5:00 p.m. on weekdays, I researched other places that could use our network during our downtimes. I found a nearby university that was willing to buy our available bandwidth on evenings and weekends.

"As a result, I designed and installed a new network that reduced downtime by 97% over the next three years. Plus, that network cost 40% less than the network our school district's IT department originally recommended."

Write your answer to this question here.

SITUATION: _____
_____

TASK: _____
_____

ACTIONS: _____
_____
_____
_____
_____
_____
_____
_____
_____
_____
_____

RESULT: _____
_____
_____

Fit Question #5:
Tell Me About a Time When You Demonstrated Persistence

Here's Billy's answer to this question in an education interview:

"I'm a volunteer basketball coach for the Boys & Girls Club. My main task is to teach kids to work tougher in teams. That was particularly difficult last year when I had a few boys who really didn't get along with each other.

"I tried everything I could find in coaching manuals and books about teamwork. I tried to define shared goals, create a culture of cooperation, and open up lines of communication. Nothing worked. Two of the boys were particularly challenging as they fought during nearly every practice. Finally, I got their parents' permission to take those two boys on a field trip together. We went on an eight hour hike, which was grueling. Near the end of the hike, they finally let down their guards and started talking to each other. They learned that they had some similar interests, and they even exchanged phone numbers at the end of the day.

"As a result of my persistence, those two boys have become best friends. Because I wouldn't give up on them, they've learned to work together, and they've become two of the best players on a winning basketball team."

Write your answer to this question here.

SITUATION: _____
_____

TASK: _____
_____

ACTIONS: _____
_____
_____
_____
_____
_____
_____
_____
_____
_____
_____

RESULT: _____
_____
_____

REFERENCE MATERIALS

Step 7: Practice the Case Questions

In this section, I've included commonly asked case questions, a great answer to each question, and templates for you to record your own answers.

Case Question #1:
If Your Brand's Sales Start to Decline,
What Would You Do?

Here's Jim's answer to this question in a marketing interview:

"I'd start with the 3C's, and then I'd move on to the 4P's.

"First, I'd start with my customers. Have there been any changes in their purchasing behavior or their preferences that are impacting my sales? Then, I'd look at competitors. Have any of them launched any new products or changed their promotional strategies recently. Next, I'd look at my company. Have we changed the way we've prioritized our brands or have we reallocated resources across our initiatives?

"Then, I'd look at the 4P's. Have my products changed in any way? For example, did I reformulate anything? Next, I'd ask if I changed my pricing strategy. Am I charging more for my products than I used to? Then, I'd look at my promotions. Have I changed my marketing message or tactics recently? Finally, I'd look at the placement of my products. Have I lost distribution, or am I losing shelf space in stores?

"Once I asked those questions, I'd assess what's happening to cause my brand's sales to decline. Then, I'd formulate a strategy to get my brand back on track."

Write your answer to this question here.

FRAMEWORK: _____

_____

ANSWER: _____

_____
_____
_____
_____
_____
_____
_____
_____
_____
_____
_____
_____
_____
_____
_____
_____
_____

REFERENCE MATERIALS

Case Question #2:
You Have a Patient Who Faints. What Do You Do?

Here's Sarah's answer to this question in a healthcare interview:

"For fainting, I'd use a mnemonic that I learned called L.A.R.C.

"First, I'd lay the person flat on their back. That's the L. Then, I'd check their airway, which is the A. If they weren't breathing, I'd administer CPR. Next, I'd try to revive them, which is the R. I could do that by tapping on their arm and talking to them loudly. If that didn't work, I'd call for help. That's the C.

"If at any time, they started to vomit, I'd turn them on their side so they don't swallow the vomit. If they regained consciousness, I would check to see if they might be dehydrated or if they might not have eaten in a while. If that were the case, I might try to get them to drink some water or some juice.

"Finally, I'd stay with them until they were fully recovered or until help arrived."

Write your answer to this question here.

FRAMEWORK: _____

_____

ANSWER: _____

_____

_____

_____

_____

_____

_____

_____

_____

_____

_____

_____

_____

_____

_____

_____

_____

_____

REFERENCE MATERIALS

Case Question #3:
If I Asked You to Design a New Highway Intersection, How Would You Approach That?

Here's Abby's answer to this question in an engineering interview:

"I'd use a process that I've learned called SOLVE. It stands for Study the problem, Organize the facts, Line up the plan, Verify the plan, and Examine the answer.

"Here's how it works. First, I'd study the intersection to find any issues or opportunities for improving it. Then, I'd organize facts like how much space I had to work with, how the traffic currently flowed through the intersection, and what the future needs might be. Then, I'd line up a plan, which could involve designing the number of lanes and whether stoplights might be needed. Then, I'd verify the plan by calculating whether my new design would improve the traffic flow. Finally, I'd examine my answer to make sure my assumptions and calculations were correct. Once I did all that, I'd show my plan to a few traffic experts to see if they could find any ways to improve it."

Write your answer to this question here.

FRAMEWORK: _____
_____

ANSWER: _____
_____
_____
_____
_____
_____
_____
_____
_____
_____
_____
_____
_____
_____
_____
_____
_____

Case Question #4:
If Your Boss Asked You to Debug a Program,
How Would You Approach It?

Here's Ethan's answer to this question in a computer science interview:

"I'd use a process that I call re-scuffed. It stands for Recognize that a bug exists, find the Source of the bug, identify the Cause, determine the Fix, and Test the fix.

"Recognizing that a bug exists would be the easy part since my boss has asked me to fix it. To find the source, I'd test the program to see where it stops working when the bug occurs. Then, I'd find the cause of the bug by going into the source code to see where the program might be faulty. Then, I'd determine the fix by writing updated source code that is bug-free. Finally, I'd test the fix by re-running the program after I inserted the new code. If everything works, then I would have successfully debugged the program. If not, I'd go back to the beginning and do the re-scuffed process again until I fixed the error."

Write your answer to this question here.

FRAMEWORK: _____

_____

ANSWER: _____

_____
_____
_____
_____
_____
_____
_____
_____
_____
_____
_____
_____
_____
_____
_____
_____

Case Question #5:
How Would You Handle a Parent Who
Wants Constant Updates on Their Child's Progress?

Here's Billy's answer to this question in an education interview:

"I'd use a technique called ASKE, which is spelled A.S.K.E. The A stands for Assume positive intent. S is for Seek to understand. K means Keep looking for an acceptable solution, and E means Elevate when needed.

"I'd start by assuming that the parent has positive intentions. They might want to ensure that their child is getting a good education and making the progress that they should be making. Next, I'd seek to understand why the parent wanted such frequent updates. I'd meet with the parents and ask them about any concerns they may have. Then, I'd keep working with them to find an acceptable solution. I'd reassure the parents about our teaching techniques and their child's progress. I'd also see if there was a way I could update them frequently enough to meet their needs without it becoming unreasonable for their child or for me. If the issue continued, I'd elevate the issue by getting input from other teachers who have more experience than I have. If necessary, I might even elevate the issue to the school's principal to see if they had any suggestions."

Write your answer to this question here.

FRAMEWORK: _____
_____

ANSWER: _____
_____
_____
_____
_____
_____
_____
_____
_____
_____
_____
_____
_____
_____
_____
_____
_____
_____
_____

REFERENCE MATERIALS

Step 8: Nail the Interviews

Here's your checklist for nailing your interviews:

____ Complete steps 1 through 7 in this book.

____ Network with the recruiters on your Job Hunting Strategy list.

____ Work with your career development office to get interviews with those recruiters.

____ Go to bed early the night before your interview, and get a good night's sleep.

____ If you have a morning interview, wake up early, eat a full breakfast, and arrive at your interview 15 minutes before your scheduled time.

____ Relax, look over your resume, and mentally think through your best interview answers.

____ When it's your time for your interview, greet the recruiter with a smile and a firm handshake.

____ Nail the interview! This should be easy given all the preparation you've done.

____ At the end of the interview, thank the recruiter and tell them how interested you are in the job.

____ Follow up with a short, polite email to the recruiter thanking them for their time and reiterating your interest in the job.

Acknowledgements

I'd like to thank my lovely wife who gave me the idea for this book and encouragement throughout the writing process. She's also supported me over the years while I've traveled to college campuses to interview job candidates and lead interview training workshops.

I'd also like to thank my twelve-year-old daughter. She provided the first round of proofreading for this book at a very reasonable rate. Hopefully, some of the tips in this book will stick with her, and she'll be able to impress recruiters someday as a result.

I'm also thankful for Eric Bishop, my co-author for my first book. He introduced me to Fiverr.com, Freelancer.com, and other tools that have been invaluable in the book publishing process.

About the Author

Richard Blazevich leads the campus recruiting efforts for the marketing department of a multinational consumer products company. Over the years, he has interviewed hundreds of candidates for a wide variety of roles. He has also led interview workshops for career development offices and student organizations at some of the top universities in the United States.

Richard is a senior director of marketing with over fifteen years of experience. He received an MBA with an emphasis in Marketing and Business Strategy from the University of Michigan and a Bachelor's degree in Business from Montana State University.

ABOUT THE AUTHOR

If you've enjoyed this book, here are other books by this author you might want to read.

Amazing Interview Answers

In this book, you'll find a list of 44 common interview questions along with winning answers for each question. You'll also get frameworks for preparing your interview answers and tips for researching jobs. If you're the type of person who learns by example, this book is for you.

Start-to-Finish Resume Guide

Discover how to write a winning resume. Get step-by-step instructions for building the perfect resume for the job you want. You'll learn tricks like key word stuffing and rapid customization to give you a competitive advantage in even the most challenging job market.

Start-to-Finish Job Search Guide

Learn everything you'll need to know to get your dream job. This book explains how to prepare your job search strategy, customize your resume, and nail your interviews. It contains a step-by-step plan to help you get the job you want.

That's a Bullseye

Whether you're a beginning business school student or an experienced marketer, this book provides a practical approach for creating a strategy to grow your business in an ever-changing marketplace. The authors outline six easy steps for building a powerful advertising campaign and online presence. You'll also get helpful templates you can use to hit a bullseye with your highest-potential customers.